FARMHOUSE
COOKBOOK

Written & Compiled by
Jo Anne Calabria

Photography
Ray Joyce

Illustrations
Barbara Rodanska

LEOPARD

This edition published in 1995 by Leopard Books,
a division of Random House UK Ltd,
20 Vauxhall Bridge Road, London SW1V 2SA

First published in 1991 by Murdoch Books,
a division of Murdoch Magazines Pty Ltd,
213 Miller Street, North Sydney NSW 2060

Printed by New Interlitho, Italy
Typeset by Savage Type Pty Ltd, Brisbane, Qld

ISBN 0 7529 0158 3

The publisher thanks the following for their assistance in the
photography for this book:

Accoutrement Cook Shop
Country Floors
Hale Imports
Horgan Imports
Royal Doulton
Toad Hall Antiques and Decor
Villeroy and Boch
Wardlaw Pty Ltd
Waterford Wedgwood

A NOTE TO COOKS

The recipes in this book use a combination of metric weights
and, for some dry and liquid ingredients, cup measures.
Cooks wishing to use Imperial weights, or who are
unfamiliar with cup measures, should consult the
Conversion Chart before attempting any of the recipes.

COOKERY RATING

easy

a little care needed

for confident cooks

CONTENTS

CONVERSION CHART

WEIGHTS AND MEASURES

Australian and American cooks use standard measuring cups for liquids and many solids, including flour, sugar, cocoa powder and prepared vegetables and fruits, whereas British cooks favour measuring jugs calibrated in millilitres and fluid ounces and scales calibrated in both metric and Imperial measures. The chart that follows gives equivalent metric, Imperial and standard cup measures. Please note that an American pint is equivalent to 16 fl oz whereas a British pint is 20 fl oz.

LIQUID MEASURES

Metric	Imperial	Standard Cup Measure
30 mL	1 fl oz	
60 mL	2 fl oz	¼ cup
75 mL	2½ fl oz	
80 mL	2¾ fl oz	⅓ cup
90 mL	3 fl oz	
125 mL	4 fl oz	½ cup
155 mL	5 fl oz	
170 mL	5½ fl oz	⅔ cup
185 mL	6 fl oz	¾ cup
220 mL	7 fl oz	
250 mL	8 fl oz	1 cup (½ US pint)
280 mL	9 fl oz	
315 mL	10 fl oz (½ pint)	1¼ cups
350 mL	11 fl oz	1⅓ cups
375 mL	12 fl oz	1½ cups
410 mL	13 fl oz	1⅔ cups
440 mL	14 fl oz	1¾ cups
470 mL	15 fl oz	
500 mL	16 fl oz	2 cups (1 US pint)
600 mL	20 fl oz (1 pint)	2½ cups
750 mL	1 pint 5 fl oz	3 cups
1 litre	1 pint 12 fl oz	4 cups
1.5 litres	2 pints 8 fl oz	6 cups

DRY MEASURES

Metric	Imperial
15 g	½ oz
30 g	1 oz
45 g	1½ oz
60 g	2 oz
90 g	3 oz
125 g	4 oz
155 g	5 oz
185 g	6 oz
220 g	7 oz
250 g	8 oz
280 g	9 oz
315 g	10 oz
350 g	11 oz
375 g	12 oz
410 g	13 oz
440 g	14 oz
470 g	15 oz
500 g	16 oz (1 lb)
750 g	1 lb 8 oz (1½ lb)
1 kg	2¼ lb
1.5 kg	3¼ lb
2 kg	4½ lb
2.5 kg	5½ lb

STANDARD CUP MEASURES

It is not possible to give a single standard cup measure for all dry ingredients as they all weigh different amounts; a cup of breadcrumbs, for instance, weighs 60 g/2 oz, whereas a cup of sugar weighs 250 g/8 oz. Some of the more common ingredients traditionally measured by cup in America and/or Australia are listed below:

Cup Measures	Metric/Imperial
1 cup butter or margarine (2 US sticks)	250 g/8 oz
1 cup grated hard cheese	125 g/4 oz
1 cup cream cheese/full fat soft cheese	250 g/8 oz
1 cup crumbled blue vein cheese	125–155 g/4–5 oz
1 cup plain/all-purpose flour	125 g/4 oz
1 cup wholemeal/wholewheat flour	140 g/4½ oz
1 cup crystalline/granulated sugar	250 g/8 oz
1 cup caster/superfine sugar	250 g/8 oz
1 cup icing/confectioners' sugar	155 g/5 oz
1 cup packed brown sugar	185 g/6 oz
1 cup chopped nuts	125 g/4 oz
1 cup soft/fresh breadcrumbs	60 g/2 oz
1 cup dry breadcrumbs	125 g/4 oz
1 cup raw rice	220 g/7 oz
1 cup cooked rice	125 g/4 oz
1 cup desiccated coconut	90 g/3 oz
1 cup cornflakes	25 g/1 oz
1 cup dried fruit (types vary)	155–185 g/5–6 oz
1 cup cooked mashed pumpkin	350 g/11 oz
1 cup pasta shapes	125 g/4 oz
1 cup chopped tomatoes	185 g/6 oz
1 cup chopped onion	125 g/4 oz
1 cup chopped capsicum/sweet pepper	125 g/4 oz
1 cup sliced mushrooms	125 g/4 oz
1 cup shelled peas	170 g/5½ oz
1 cup diced raw potato	185 g/6 oz
1 cup mashed potato	250 g/8 oz
1 cup diced apple	125 g/4 oz
1 cup apple purée (applesauce)	250 g/8 oz
1 cup black or redcurrants or blueberries	125 g/4 oz
1 cup raspberries or small strawberries	155 g/5 oz
1 cup honey, syrup or jam	350–375 g/11–12 oz
1 cup minced/ground beef or pork	250 g/8 oz

STANDARD SPOON MEASURES

When measuring by teaspoon (tsp) or tablespoon (tbsp), always use standard metric measuring spoons. While these are the same for Britain and the US (5 mL and 15 mL respectively), please note that the Australian standard tablespoon holds 20 mL and is therefore equivalent to 4 standard teaspoons. As recipes for this book were tested in Australia, British and American readers will need to adjust tablespoon quantities.

Australia	UK	US
1 tsp (5 mL)	1 tsp (5 mL)	1 tsp (5 mL)
1 tbsp (20 mL)	1 tbsp (15 mL)	1 tbsp (15 mL)

LINEAR MEASURES

5 mm	¼ in
1 cm	½ in
2 cm	¾ in
2.5 cm	1 in
5 cm	2 in
6 cm	2½ in
8 cm	3 in
10 cm	4 in
12 cm	5 in
15 cm	6 in
18 cm	7 in
20 cm	8 in
23 cm	9 in
25 cm	10 in
28 cm	11 in
30 cm	12 in
46 cm	18 in
50 cm	20 in
61 cm	24 in
77 cm	30 in

OVEN TEMPERATURES

	°C	°F	Gas Mark
Very slow	120	250	½
Slow	150	300	1–2
Mod. slow	160	325	3
Moderate	180	350	4
Mod. hot	190	375	5–6
Hot	200	400	6–7
Very hot	230	450	8–9

Soups

ABIG POT OF SOUP simmering on the stove or by the fireside was a familiar sight in farmhouse kitchens of the past. For thousands of years, peasant families in many countries thrived on such simple fare, sometimes eaten with bread and cheese. In today's world soup is as popular as ever it was. Serve it as a meal in itself or as the first course of a special menu. Ladle your fill from the tureens of heart-warming brews we have gathered for you here. They come from Britain, Russia, the Mediterranean, the Middle East and India — and they're all delicious.

Piquant Three-Meat Soup and Split Pea Soup with Meatballs (page 10)

Split Pea Soup with Meatballs

Legumes are filling because they contain a large amount of fibre — great for maintaining a healthy lifestyle.

A complete meal in a bowl — an excellent luncheon dish on a cold winter's day. Do not make meatballs too large; they should be able to be just popped into the mouth. The soup should be made the day before required to allow flavours to develop.

PREPARATION TIME: 1½ hours
COOKING TIME: 30 minutes
SERVES 6

2 cups green split peas
1.5 L chicken stock or water
½ cup chopped celery
1 large onion, chopped
½ teaspoon dried marjoram
¼ teaspoon pepper
500 g pork and veal mince
2 rashers bacon, chopped
2 tablespoons chopped parsley
2 teaspoons grated lemon rind
½ teaspoon dried sage
3 potatoes, peeled and diced
juice of 1 lemon

1 Wash split peas in cold water. Drain and put in large pot, and add chicken stock or water, celery, onion, marjoram and pepper. Bring to the boil. Reduce heat, cover and simmer for 1 hour or until peas are tender. Do not drain.
2 Combine pork and veal mince, bacon, parsley, lemon rind and sage. Mix well with hand. Using wetted hands, shape into walnut-sized balls.
3 Gently drop meatballs and potatoes into soup mixture. Return soup to boiling. Reduce heat, cover and simmer for 20–30 minutes or until meatballs and potatoes are cooked. Add lemon juice to taste.

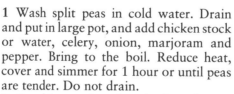

Piquant Three-Meat Soup

A thick, hearty Russian soup. It has a sharp but sweet flavour that blends well with the addition of a spoonful of sour cream to each serve. A very rich beef stock is required for the base of this soup. Canned beef consommé can be used, made up to the required amount with water.

PREPARATION TIME: 20 minutes
COOKING TIME: 1¼ hours
SERVES 6

1 tablespoon olive oil
1 large onion, chopped
500 g topside steak, fat removed, cut into small cubes
125 g kassler (smoked pork) cut into cubes
125 g cabanossi, sliced into rounds
¼ small cabbage, shredded
1 L rich beef stock
1 x 440 g can peeled tomatoes
2 tablespoons brown sugar
2 tablespoons malt vinegar
½ cup chopped sweet and sour cucumbers
1 tablespoon chopped capers
¾ cup thick sour cream
¼ cup chopped fresh dill

1 Heat oil in large saucepan. Add onion, fry 2 minutes and add cubed topside. Cook 5–7 minutes or until well browned.
2 Add kassler, cabanossi and cabbage and fry for 2–3 minutes. Pour over stock and tomatoes. Place lid on pan and cook over low heat for 45 minutes.
3 Add brown sugar, vinegar, cucumber and capers. Stir to combine; cook further 7–10 minutes.
4 Serve in deep soup bowls topped with a spoonful of sour cream. Sprinkle with chopped dill.

Split Pea Soup with Meatballs

Summer Vegetable Soup

Take advantage of seasonal tomatoes while they are at their best. Summer tomatoes are sweet and juicy, giving plenty of flavour to this Mediterranean soup.

PREPARATION TIME: *30 minutes*
COOKING TIME: *60 minutes*
SERVES 6

2 tablespoons olive oil
2 cloves garlic, crushed
2 red onions, diced
1 red capsicum, diced
300 g fresh tomatoes, skinned and chopped
2 tablespoons chopped chives
half a small cabbage, shredded
fresh thyme leaves
200 g button mushrooms, sliced
400 mL tomato juice
1 cup water
1 tablespoon sugar
1 tablespoon wine vinegar
1 tablespoon tomato paste
pepper
chopped chives for garnish

1 Heat oil, add garlic, onions and capsicum and cook, stirring until onion is transparent.
2 Add tomatoes, chives, cabbage, thyme and mushrooms. Cover and simmer gently 15 minutes.
3 Pour over tomato juice, water, sugar, vinegar, tomato paste and pepper. Simmer uncovered 30 minutes. Remove any scum as it forms on the surface. Serve hot, sprinkled with chives.

Summer Vegetable Soup

1 Heat oil, add garlic, diced onions and capsicum and cook, stirring until onion is transparent, about 6–8 minutes.

2 Peel tomatoes by making a small cut in the skin and covering them with boiling water. Use a sharp knife to peel skin away.

3 Add peeled tomatoes, chives, cabbage, thyme and mushrooms to pan. Simmer gently 15 minutes.

4 Remove any scum that forms on the surface with a large metal spoon.

Peeling tomatoes is very simple if you cook on gas. Place a ripe, firm tomato core end-on to the prongs of a fork and rotate over gas flame until the skin bursts; it will make a squealing sound. Remove skin using sharp knife.

There are many forms of edible fungi but the most abundant kind are cultivated mushrooms. They are sold as button mushrooms (small unopened caps with a delicate flavour), caps or cups (mushrooms that are opened with a slightly stronger flavour) and open flats, which are the large flat mushrooms with a rich full flavour. All mushrooms are best stored in brown paper bags in the refrigerator. Never peel mushrooms but wipe them with a damp cloth. Leave whole or slice as required.

Celeriac and Stilton Soup

Stilton is a blue-mould cheese originating in Stilton, Huntingdonshire. It marries well with the celeriac or celery to give this creamy puréed soup.

PREPARATION TIME: *30 minutes*
COOKING TIME: *45 minutes*
SERVES 4–6

125 g butter
2 heads celeriac, peeled and chopped
¼ cup chopped chives
3 tablespoons finely chopped basil
⅓ cup plain flour
1.25 L chicken stock
350 g Stilton cheese
pepper to taste
croûtons and basil to serve

1 Melt butter in a large heavy-based pan. Add celeriac, cover and simmer over medium heat for 10 minutes. Add basil and chives, cover and simmer a further 5 minutes.
2 Remove from heat and blend in flour until smooth. Stir in 1 L chicken stock. Return to heat and simmer, stirring until mixture comes to the boil; reduce heat and simmer 15 minutes.
3 Crumble cheese, place in a blender or food processor with remaining stock and blend to form a smooth paste. Add cheese mixture to soup, stir and bring back to the boil. Simmer 10 minutes.
4 Serve in heated soup bowls garnished with small basil leaves and accompanied with croûtons.

Stilton is one of the world's great blue cheeses. This rich milk cheese is made only in the months from May to September in the English Midlands towns of Derbyshire and Leicestershire from whole milk and cream. Steel needles are pushed into the cheese to develop the characteristic blue mould. After four to six months ripening a brown crusty rind covers the cheese and it's ready to enjoy.
Stilton has a rich, pungent flavour, so serve it with a good port at the end of a meal or enrich sauces, soups and quiches with its flavour.

Chicken Soup with Lemon and Garlic

Every culture has its chicken soup. This one has been derived from the Middle East. It has a strong garlic and lemon flavour. Rice is used as the thickening agent; more or less may be added depending on personal preference.

PREPARATION TIME: *15 minutes*
COOKING TIME: *1½ hours*
SERVES 4

1 x 1 kg chicken, skin and fat removed
2 L water
1 onion, quartered
2 long strips lemon rind
1 tablespoon oil or butter
3 cloves garlic
4 stalks celery
1 leek, sliced
⅓ cup chopped coriander
½ cup lemon juice — about 2 lemons
1 cup cooked long-grain rice
1 L water, extra

1 Place prepared chicken in large pan, cover with water and add onion and lemon rind. Bring to boil, cover and cook for 1–1½ hours or until chicken is tender.
2 Remove chicken from stock. Strain stock and reserve. Remove chicken meat from bone and shred or chop finely.
3 Heat oil in large pan. Add garlic, celery and leek and cook covered over low heat until celery and leek have softened. Add reserved stock and prepared chicken meat, coriander, lemon juice, rice and extra water. Bring to boil, cook for 3–4 minutes and season to taste.
4 Serve hot, garnished with extra coriander.

Celeriac and Stilton Soup

Celeriac and Stilton Soup and Chicken Soup with Lemon and Garlic

Curry Rice Soup (page 15), Hearty Pork and Bean Soup and Potato Bacon Soup

Potato Bacon Soup with Cheese Strips

A quick, easy-to-make soup, ideal as a winter luncheon dish. If potatoes are allowed to stand, cover with cold water to prevent browning. Drain well before using.

PREPARATION TIME: *20 minutes*
COOKING TIME: *15 minutes*
SERVES 6

1 tablespoon olive oil
1 large onion, *chopped*
4 rashers bacon, *chopped*
4 large potatoes, *peeled and grated*
1.2 L chicken or vegetable stock
½ teaspoon ground thyme
¼ teaspoon nutmeg
6 slices thick white bread, *crust removed*
2 tablespoons olive oil, *extra*
1 cup freshly grated Parmesan cheese
basil leaves for garnish

1 Heat oil in saucepan, add onion and bacon and cook until golden brown. Add potato, stock, thyme and nutmeg and bring to the boil. Reduce to simmer, cover and cook 15 minutes.
2 Brush bread on both sides with olive oil, spread with Parmesan cheese and cut into 4 strips. Place on baking tray and bake at 180°C for 7–10 minutes until golden brown.
3 Serve soup garnished with basil and accompanied by cheese strips.
Note: Cheese strips may be prepared up to baking stage. Place in container in single layer, cover and freeze. They may be cooked straight from the freezer.

Hearty Pork and Bean Soup

A thick, rich-flavoured soup that requires long, slow cooking for full flavour to develop. Choose lean pork — pork medallions or fillet would be suitable.

Content

PREPARATION TIME: *30 minutes*
COOKING TIME: *1½ hours*
SERVES 4–6

1 tablespoon olive oil
2 cloves garlic, crushed
1 large onion, chopped
6 rashers lean bacon, chopped
250 g boneless pork, fat removed, diced
2 large ripe tomatoes, peeled and chopped
1 stick celery, chopped
1 carrot, chopped
½ small cabbage, shredded
½ fennel bulb, chopped
2 teaspoons fresh thyme or ½ teaspoon dried thyme
1.5 L chicken stock
2 x 310 g cans mixed beans, drained

1 Heat oil in large pan, add garlic and onion and fry 1 minute.
2 Add bacon and pork and cook over medium heat until pork is well browned. Add prepared vegetables, thyme and stock. Cover pan, bring to the boil, reduce heat and simmer for 1¼ hours.
3 Add beans and cook further 15 minutes.
4 Serve hot with crusty bread.

Curry Rice Soup

A spicy Indian-style soup originating from the days of the British Raj in India. The soup can be as thick or thin as you desire by changing the amount of cooked rice, or as hot or spicy as you like by altering the quantity of spices.

PREPARATION TIME: *10 minutes*
COOKING TIME: *25 minutes*
SERVES 4–6

60 g butter
2 large onions, chopped
2 teaspoons curry powder
1 teaspoon turmeric
½ teaspoon ground cardamom
½ teaspoon ground cumin
2 tablespoons flour
1.2 L beef stock
grated rind of 1 lemon
1 cup cooked rice

½ cup coconut milk
1 lemon, quartered, for serving

1 Melt butter in large saucepan, add onion and cook gently 3–4 minutes. Stir in curry powder, turmeric, cardamom and cumin; fry 2–3 minutes.
2 Remove from heat, add flour and gradually stir in beef stock. Return to heat, stirring constantly until mixture boils and thickens. Reduce heat and simmer, covered, for 15 minutes.
3 Stir in lemon rind, rice and coconut milk and heat for 5 minutes.
4 Serve accompanied by lemon wedges.

Fennel and Apple Soup

A light refreshing soup, a perfect start to a heavier meal. Fennel is from the bulb family of vegetables; it has a sweet anise-like flavour that blends particularly well with the sharpness of green apples.

PREPARATION TIME: *30 minutes*
COOKING TIME: *45 minutes*
SERVES 4

2 large fennel bulbs
2 tablespoons olive oil
2 cloves garlic, crushed
2 large green apples, peeled, cored and chopped
1 L chicken stock
4 rounds thickly sliced French bread
2 tablespoons olive oil, extra
1 tablespoon fennel seeds

1 Remove outer parts of fennel bulbs and slice tender interior into fine strips.
2 Heat oil in pan, add garlic, gently cook 1 minute and add prepared fennel and apple. Place lid on pan, reduce to low heat and allow to cook until fennel and apple are soft but not browned.
3 Add chicken stock, cover and cook for 45 minutes.
4 Brush bread rounds with oil on both sides. Place on baking tray and sprinkle with fennel seeds. Place in oven for 5–7 minutes or until golden brown. To serve, place piece of bread in each soup bowl, ladle in soup and serve immediately.

Fennel and Apple Soup

Croûtons are small rounds or decorative shapes of bread that are toasted or fried until golden and used to garnish soups and salads. Croûtes are larger rounds or squares of fried or toasted bread that are used to accompany game dishes and some casseroles.

STOCKS

Whatever soup, sauce or stew you are making it will taste decidedly better if its base is a home-made stock or broth. The basic method of preparing stock is much the same for meat, poultry, fish and vegetables: simply simmer all the ingredients until their full flavours are released. There are, though, some essential points to follow when making stock.

Essential Points
Use a large heavy-based saucepan with a well-fitting lid to allow your stock to simmer evenly.

Choose the freshest ingredients for your base and make use of meat or poultry trimmings, bones, carcasses and clean vegetable trimmings.

Bring the stock to the boil very slowly without stirring as this lessens the chance of a cloudy stock.

As soon as the stock comes to the boil reduce the heat and simmer gently for about 3–4 hours to release all the essential flavours.

Add aromatic herbs and vegetables to stockpot in the last hour of cooking — this stops the vegetables overcooking and clouding the stock.

Remove any white scum that rises while the stock is simmering.

When the stock is cooked, carefully strain the liquid through a fine sieve, taking care not to disturb the solid ingredients to avoid clouding the stock.

When the stock is cool remove any fat with absorbent paper, cover and refrigerate. After refrigeration any remaining fat will solidify and can easily be lifted off.

Stock will store for up to one week under refrigeration and for up to four months in the freezer.

Stock must always be brought to the boil again before use in soups, sauces and stews.

Basic Stocks

For a basic stock you will need about 500 g of solid ingredients and about 2 L water to make 1.5 L stock.

Beef Stock Use stewing beef. Shin and oxtail are tasty and add natural gelatin to thicken the stock slightly. Any meat trimmings, chicken carcasses, wings or wing tips are also good. Add large pieces of carrot, leek, whole onions and unpeeled garlic cloves (peeled garlic cooks to a purée and clouds the stock). A bouquet garni of bay leaf, thyme, parsley and marjoram can also be added.

Chicken Stock A large boiling bird is best used for a full-flavoured stock. Add any other chicken trimmings you may have, including giblets and neck. Carrots, celery, garlic and a whole onion studded with a few cloves give depth of flavour, as will bay leaves and parsley.

Fish Stock Use fish heads, carcasses and trimmings for fish stock and cook for only about 45 minutes. Add onion, fennel, thyme, parsley and lemon rind without pith for extra flavour. Fish stock has little or no fat and is less clear than meat stocks. Use within one day or freeze for later use.

Vegetable Stock Vegetable stock also needs a short cooking time, only 40–45 minutes simmering to release essential flavours. Any longer and the vegetables begin to disintegrate and cloud the stock. Use carrots, leek, celery, parsley, onion and cabbage, chopped into small even-sized pieces to yield the most flavour.

Coarse salt and whole peppercorns may be added to the stockpot if desired to add flavour. Ground pepper should only be added to the final dish, never to the base stock as long slow cooking with pepper results in a sharp and harsh aftertaste.

1 Pack a large heavy-based saucepan with your choice of meat bones, carcasses and trimmings.

2 Bring the stock to the boil very slowly. Then simmer for about 4 hours. Remove any scum that forms.

3 In the last hour of cooking add your choice of aromatic vegetables — try carrot, celery and onion.

4 Add a bouquet garni to the stockpot to give flavour. A whole onion studded with cloves is also good.

5 Carefully strain stock, taking care not to disturb the solid ingredients to avoid clouding the liquid.

6 Cool stock to room temperature and remove any excess fat with absorbent kitchen paper.

7 After refrigeration remove any solidified fat with a metal spoon. Ice cubes can be added to stock to solidify the fat quickly.

8 Stock will keep for up to one week under refrigeration and for up to 4 months if frozen. Try freezing stock in ice cube trays.

Pasta, Rice & Egg Dishes

Here are some earthy old-style temptations based on ingredients which have survived to stimulate our palates today. Grains from the harvest and eggs from the henhouse are beloved traditional foods in all countries. Take your choice from the risottos and other rice dishes; the pastas teamed with vegetables and light meats; and the intriguing egg-based meals on the pages which follow. Savour their enticing aromas and flavours, so economical and easy to prepare, and take them to your table to share with your family and friends with pride.

Clockwise from top right: Onion Tart, Penne with Basil and Pancetta (page 21)
and Risotto with Seasonal Vegetables (page 20)

Butter and oil are the perfect combination when shallow frying. Butter gives you the flavour and oil gives you the heating quality.

Risotto with Seasonal Vegetables

Not only does this recipe taste great, it also has a colourful appearance from the combination of vegetables and the addition of saffron. Saffron threads are best soaked in water before using. Add threads and soaking water to recipe.

PREPARATION TIME: *20 minutes*
COOKING TIME: *30 minutes*
SERVES 4–6

2 tablespoons butter
2 tablespoons olive oil
1 large onion, chopped
1½ cups long-grain rice
2½ cups chicken stock
¼ teaspoon powdered saffron or saffron threads
3 large firm, slightly underripe, tomatoes, chopped
3 large zucchini, chopped
1 small green capsicum, diced
1 small red capsicum, diced
1 cup finely grated Parmesan cheese to serve

1 Heat butter over medium heat in large heavy-based saucepan; add oil. Add chopped onion and cook 2 minutes. Add rice and cook until golden brown. Add the chicken stock, saffron and prepared vegetables.
2 Bring rice mixture to the boil and allow to boil 5–7 minutes, then reduce to very low heat. Place lid on saucepan and cook for further 10–12 minutes or until rice is tender. Serve hot with Parmesan cheese.

1 Heat butter in a heavy-based saucepan, add oil and onion and cook for 2 minutes. Add the rice and cook, stirring, until rice is lightly golden.

2 To ensure maximum colour and flavour from saffron threads, lightly toast them in a small pan and dissolve the threads in warm water before adding to rice.

Saffron consists of the bright orange-red stigmas of the saffron crocus. It is the most expensive spice in the world owing to the labour-intensive harvesting of the spice; it takes between two hundred thousand and four hundred thousand stigmas to produce 450 grams of saffron. Saffron is an essential ingredient in Spanish Paella and Provençal Bouillabaisse.

3 Bring rice and vegetable mixture to the boil and allow mixture to boil for 5–7 minutes or until small tunnels form. Reduce heat and cook covered 10 minutes.

4 Use the large holes of the grater for freshly grated Parmesan cheese. Grated Parmesan stores well in an airtight container in the refrigerator.

Onion Tart

Spanish onions have a delicate flavour and purplish flesh. They combine with the leeks to give the characteristic flavours in this quiche. If Spanish onions are unavailable, use white rather than brown onions.

PREPARATION TIME: *45 minutes*
COOKING TIME: *30 minutes*
MAKES *1 x 20 cm tart*

PASTRY
2 cups plain flour
½ teaspoon salt
2 tablespoons Parmesan cheese
150 g butter
water to bind, about 3 tablespoons
FILLING
500 g red Spanish onions
2 leeks
50 mL olive oil
1 tablespoon red wine vinegar
250 g Swiss cheese, grated
½ cup cream
¾ cup milk
3 eggs
¼ cup chopped parsley
¼ teaspoon freshly grated nutmeg

1 Sift flour, salt and Parmesan cheese together into a bowl and rub in the butter until mixture resembles fine breadcrumbs. Add sufficient water to bring pastry together. Knead lightly and refrigerate 10 minutes.
2 Roll out pastry and line a 20 cm pie plate or quiche pan with the prepared pastry. Bake blind at 210°C for 10 minutes. Allow to cool.
3 Peel and thinly slice onions; wash and thinly slice the leeks. Heat oil in a heavy-based pan and cook the onions till soft. Add vinegar and leeks, cover and cook 5 minutes on medium heat.
4 Lightly beat cream, milk and eggs together; add parsley and seasonings. Scatter half cheese over pastry base and add half the cooked onion mixture. Repeat with remaining cheese and onion mixture. Pour over combined liquid ingredients.
5 Bake at 170°C for about 30 minutes or until cooked and custard has set. Serve warm or cold.

Penne with Basil and Pancetta

Smoked pancetta comes in two varieties, hot or mild. Either can be used for the following recipe.

PREPARATION TIME: *30 minutes*
COOKING TIME: *15 minutes*
SERVES 6

1 teaspoon olive oil
2 red capsicums
60 g butter
1 large clove garlic, crushed
1 bunch chives
400 g pancetta, cut into strips
¼ cup chopped fresh basil
500 g penne pasta
1 tablespoon olive oil
100 g freshly grated Parmesan cheese
2 tablespoons cream
fresh basil sprigs for garnish

1 Lightly rub capsicums with olive oil and bake in a hot oven (220°C) for 10 minutes, until skin on capsicums blisters. Remove from oven and cool. Remove core and seeds, skin capsicums and finely chop.
2 Heat butter in a pan, add garlic and fry until brown. Add chives and pancetta and fry 1 minute. Add basil and chopped capsicum. Remove from heat and keep warm.
3 Bring a large pan of water to the boil and add 1 tablespoon olive oil. When boiling rapidly add penne. Cook until pasta is *al dente*, about 10 minutes.
4 Drain immediately. Transfer to warmed pasta dish and toss through pancetta mixture, grated Parmesan and cream. Serve immediately, garnished with basil sprigs.

Pancetta is a cured Italian pork sausage from Parma. It is salted and air-dried and can be eaten cooked or raw.

Penne with Basil and Pancetta

Pasta comes in dozens of shapes and sizes, some being more suited to a particular dish than others. There are four main classifications.

Pasta for soup includes small shapes, twirls and twists sold as pastina, stellette, rotini and anelli.

Pasta for dressing with sauce is sold as spaghetti, fettuccine, bucanti and tagliatelle, while pasta to be used for baking is usually lasagne, macaroni and rigatoni. Then there is pasta that is filled and baked or boiled, including shapes like cannelloni, tortellini and ravioli.

Summer Vegetable Pasta

The combination of summer vegetables, coppa and capers produces this well-flavoured sauce to serve over pasta.

PREPARATION TIME: *40 minutes + 40 minutes draining eggplant*
COOKING TIME: *1 hour*
SERVES 6

2 red capsicums
1 tablespoon olive oil
500 g young eggplant
¼ cup olive oil
2 cloves garlic
3 small red onions, sliced
2 medium carrots, diced
1 cup chopped celery
1 cup chopped spring onions
250 g mushrooms, chopped
150 g coppa
2 tablespoons capers, chopped
1 teaspoon oregano leaves
1 tablespoon tomato paste
1 x 400 g can tomato pieces
60 g pecorino cheese, grated
500 g fusilli, penne or shell pasta

1 Rub capsicum with oil and bake in a hot oven (210°C) for about 10 minutes or until skin blisters. Remove and cool, skin and remove seeds and white core. Chop into 1 cm pieces.
2 Peel and chop eggplants into 1 cm pieces, salt lightly and allow to drain in a plastic colander for about 40 minutes.
3 Heat ¼ cup oil in a heavy-based pan, add garlic, fry 1 minute then add dried eggplant and cook until eggplant browns lightly. Remove from pan and keep warm. Add onions to remaining oil in pan; fry 2 minutes. Add carrots, celery and spring onions, fry 1 minute, cover and sweat 6 minutes. Add mushrooms, stir through, cover and sweat a further 5 minutes.
4 Remove lid from saucepan and add coppa, capers, oregano leaves, tomato pieces, tomato paste and eggplant. Stir to combine well. Cook gently 30 minutes.
5 Cook pasta according to directions on package. Drain. Toss pecorino cheese through sauce mixture. Spoon over drained pasta and serve immediately.

Vegetable and Lentil Pilau

Pilau dishes can be made of meat, vegetables, nuts, herbs and spices. The base consists of rice fried in fat and oil; then all other ingredients are added and cooked together slowly.

PREPARATION TIME: *30 minutes*
COOKING TIME: *25 minutes*
SERVES 4

1 cup long-grain rice
1 cup red lentils
60 g ghee
2 medium onions, thinly sliced
2 cloves garlic, crushed
1 red chilli, seeded and diced
2.5 cm piece green ginger, peeled and grated
2 large carrots, diced
1 large turnip, diced
½ cup chopped celery
1 tablespoon ground coriander
½ teaspoon cardamom
1 teaspoon turmeric
1 cup peas
5 cups vegetable or chicken stock, boiling

1 Wash rice and drain well. Wash lentils, removing any that float to the surface. Drain well.
2 Heat ghee in a deep saucepan. Add onions and slowly cook until they are caramel in colour (this may take as long as 20 minutes). Add garlic and chilli; cook 1 minute. Stir through ginger, carrots, turnip and celery. When vegetables have softened slightly, add coriander, cardamom and turmeric. Cook 1 minute.
3 Add rice and lentils to cooked vegetables and coat with ghee remaining in pan. Pour in boiling stock. Bring back to the boil; add peas. Cover and simmer 20–25 minutes or until lentils and rice are cooked.
Note: Do not lift the lid or stir during the cooking time. This will reduce the liquid content and cause the rice and lentils to become mushy.

Vegetable and Lentil Pilau and Summer Vegetable Pasta

Risotto with Eggplant

Risotto with Eggplant

A risotto is a rice dish cooked in stock and flavoured in many ways. Recipes vary from one area to another throughout Italy.

PREPARATION TIME: *40 minutes*
COOKING TIME: *45 minutes*
SERVES 6

1 kg eggplants
salt
1 red capsicum
1 green capsicum
400 g can Italian tomatoes
1 tablespoon olive oil
2 medium onions, chopped
1/4 cup Italian parsley, finely chopped
2 tablespoons basil, finely chopped
1 tablespoon red wine vinegar
1 tablespoon sugar
1 1/2 cups chicken stock
1 cup rice
1/2 cup dry white wine
1/4 cup olive oil, extra
60 g pecorino cheese, grated
40 g Parmesan cheese grated
250 g mozzarella cheese, grated

1 Rinse eggplant and cut into 5 mm slices lengthwise. Sprinkle with salt and stand to drain in a colander for 30 minutes. Rinse and pat dry.
2 Remove core and seeds from capsicums and finely chop. Drain and chop tomatoes, reserving juice. Heat oil in a heavy-based pan and cook onion until golden. Add capsicum and cook, stirring, 1 minute. Add tomatoes and juice, parsley, basil, vinegar and sugar. Simmer gently 10 minutes.
3 In a heavy-based pan add extra oil to cover the base and cook eggplant slices a few at a time until golden brown. Remove and drain. Continue with the remaining eggplant slices, adding some extra oil as required.
4 Add rice to simmering tomato sauce mixture and cook 5 minutes. Add wine. Cook uncovered, stirring occasionally. Keep chicken stock on the boil next to the risotto and as the liquid is absorbed, add the boiling stock. Cook until rice is just tender, about 25–30 minutes.
5 Spread rice mixture out to cool on a tray. Grease a deep ovenproof dish. Spread half the rice on base, top with half the eggplant and combined cheeses.

Continue alternating with remaining ingredients, finishing with a cheese layer.
6 Bake at 200°C for 10–12 minutes until the cheese melts and forms a brown crust. Stand 5 minutes before serving.

Farmhouse Omelette

This farmhouse-style omelette is a speciality of the Italian town of Arezzo. Serve with lots of crusty bread and green salad.

PREPARATION TIME: *20 minutes*
COOKING TIME: *30 minutes*
SERVES 4

OMELETTE
2 tablespoons olive oil
6 eggs
1 teaspoon plain flour
3 tablespoons dried breadcrumbs
SAUCE
2 tablespoons olive oil
4 rashers bacon, chopped
1/2 cup chopped spring onions
2 sticks celery, finely chopped
1 clove garlic, crushed
1 red capsicum
1 green capsicum
2 tablespoons sugar
2 x 400 g cans tomatoes

1 Heat oil in pan. Beat eggs together with flour and breadcrumbs. Pour into heated pan and cook on medium heat until almost cooked through. Turn and cook on other side 1 minute. Remove and cool. When cold, cut into thin strips.
2 Lightly oil capsicum, place on a tray and bake at 220°C for 10 minutes or until skin blisters. Remove from tray, cool, peel, remove core and seeds and finely chop capsicum flesh.
3 Drain tomatoes, reserve juice and chop the flesh.
4 Heat remaining oil in pan and fry bacon until cooked. Add spring onions, celery and garlic; fry 2 minutes. Add capsicum, sugar, tomatoes and reserved juice. Lower heat and simmer 20 minutes.
5 Add omelette strips to sauce and gently heat through before serving.

Pecorino is the Italian generic name for cheeses made of ewe's milk. The grandfather of Italian cheeses, it can be matured and used as a table cheese or dried, as in pecorino Romano, and used in place of Parmesan cheese.

Pasta with Sauce Ragù

A meat and vegetable sauce subtly flavoured with fennel is served over pasta.

PREPARATION TIME: *35 minutes*
COOKING TIME: *60 minutes*
SERVES 6

1 tablespoon olive oil
1 leek, finely chopped
1 carrot, finely chopped
2 cloves garlic, crushed
1 small fennel bulb, chopped
3 rashers bacon, rind removed, chopped
200 g chicken livers, chopped
250 g lean beef mince
250 g pork mince
1 cup white wine
1 cup milk
1 x 400 g can Italian tomatoes
¼ cup tomato purée
¼ cup chopped parsley
¼ cup basil, chopped
½ cup grated Parmesan
500 g pasta

1 Heat oil in a heavy-based pan. Add leek, carrot, garlic, fennel and bacon. Cook, stirring, for 5 minutes.

2 Add the livers, beef and pork mince to pan and cook, stirring, until light golden. Add the wine, bring to the boil and then reduce heat. Simmer uncovered until wine has evaporated. Add milk and simmer uncovered until evaporated.

3 Drain tomatoes, reserving juice, and chop tomato flesh. Add to the meat mixture with reserved juice and tomato purée. Simmer gently 45 minutes.

4 Stir through parsley and basil and simmer 5 minutes. Add Parmesan cheese when ready to serve.

5 Cook pasta in boiling water until just tender; drain. Serve on warm serving plate, topped with meat sauce.

Pasta with Sauce Ragù and Farmhouse Omelette

Rice and Beans in Red Wine and Fettuccine with Anchovies and Black Olives

Rice and Beans in Red Wine

Choose a full-bodied Italian style red wine to give the characteristic flavour to this recipe. Quick-cooking brown rice gives you the nutty flavour but only takes half the time to cook compared with ordinary brown rice.

PREPARATION TIME: *10 minutes*
COOKING TIME: *40 minutes*
SERVES 4–6

2 tablespoons butter
1 tablespoon oil
1 large onion, chopped
1½ cups quick-cooking brown rice
2½ cups chicken stock
½ cup red wine
1 x 375 g can butter beans, drained
½ cup freshly grated Parmesan cheese
Italian parsley sprigs for garnish

1 Heat butter and oil in heavy-based saucepan, add onion and rice and cook until onion is well browned.
2 Add chicken stock and red wine. Bring to the boil and boil rapidly until nearly all liquid has evaporated. Place tight-fitting lid on saucepan, reduce heat to very low and cook until rice is tender, about 30 minutes.
3 Stir in beans. Put lid back on saucepan and cook further 5 minutes.
4 Serve hot, topped with Parmesan cheese and parsley sprigs.

Fettuccine with Anchovies and Black Olives

Anchovies and olives impart a rich flavour to this pasta dish from the south of Italy.

PREPARATION TIME: *10 minutes*
COOKING TIME: *20 minutes*
SERVES 4–6

450 g green fettuccine
3 tablespoons olive oil
3 cloves garlic, crushed

6 flat anchovy fillets, drained and chopped finely
200 g black olives, stoned and chopped finely
¼ cup fresh white breadcrumbs, toasted
½ cup pimiento, drained and cut into thin strips

1 Heat oil in pan, add garlic and fry until golden brown. Add anchovies, stirring well to combine, add black olives and bread-crumbs and cook 1 minute.
2 Meanwhile cook fettuccine in large quantity boiling water. Drain.
3 Place drained fettuccine on plate, top with sauce and garnish with pimiento strips. Serve immediately, accompanied by green salad.
Note: For increased quantity and creamier flavour, add ½ cup cream to anchovy and olive sauce.

Creamy Eggs with Red Pepper

This is an ideal recipe for brunch. Do not allow the mixture to overcook or the eggs will become tough and weeping will occur. For a livelier flavour, try adding one small red chilli, cut into strips, with the onion and capsicum.

PREPARATION TIME: *10 minutes*
COOKING TIME: *10 minutes*
SERVES 4–6

1 tablespoon butter or olive oil
2 onions, sliced
2 small red capsicums, cut into thin strips
6 eggs
½ cup cream
freshly ground black pepper
chopped parsley or dill.

1 Heat butter or oil in heavy-based frying pan. Add onions and cook slowly until golden brown. Add capsicum and cook until soft.
2 Combine eggs, cream and pepper and beat until well mixed.
3 Pour mixture over onion and capsicum. Stir gently until eggs are creamy and soft.
4 Sprinkle with chopped parsley or dill and serve immediately.

The salty flavour of anchovies can be mellowed by covering them with milk and standing for thirty minutes before using. Simply drain and dry with absorbent paper and use as directed.

Creamy Eggs with Red Pepper

Persian Baked Eggs

This Persian omelette, called *Kuku*, can be baked in the oven. The vegetable selection can vary depending on what is available at the time.

PREPARATION TIME: *35 minutes*
COOKING TIME: *40–60 minutes*
SERVES 6

250 g broccoli
1 bunch silver beet, chopped
2 sticks celery, diced
8 spring onions, chopped
$^1/_2$ cup raisins
12 eggs
$^1/_4$ teaspoon freshly grated nutmeg
1 tablespoon freshly chopped dill
freshly ground pepper
$^1/_2$ cup toasted pine nuts

Pasta with Italian Sausage

1 Preheat oven to 160°C and grease a 30 × 20 cm shallow casserole dish.
2 Wash vegetables well, place broccoli florets and chopped silver beet in a lidded casserole and add one tablespoon of water. Microwave on High 5 minutes. Add celery, spring onions and raisins, cover and stand 5 minutes. If you are not using a microwave, cook vegetables in a small quantity of water until just tender.
3 Beat eggs lightly until well mixed and season with nutmeg, dill and pepper.
4 Combine vegetables with pine nuts and place in the greased casserole dish. Pour over egg mixture and bake in preheated oven for 40–60 minutes or until egg mixture has set.
5 Cut into slices to serve, garnished with sliced lemon and dill sprigs.

When cooking pasta, add cloves of garlic to water for extra flavour. To help prevent pasta from sticking together, add 2 tablespoons of olive oil to boiling water.

Pasta with Italian Sausage

This recipe uses tagliatelle — long ribbon pasta — but any pasta can be used. Try a combination of green and white.

PREPARATION TIME: *25 minutes*
COOKING TIME: *30 minutes*
SERVES 6

3 large red capsicums, cut in half, seeds removed
2 large green capsicums, cut in half, seeds removed
500 g Italian pork sausage or salami, sliced
30 g butter
1 large onion, chopped
$^3/_4$ cup red wine
$^3/_4$ cup chicken stock
1 tablespoon tomato paste
1 teaspoon sugar
freshly ground black pepper
500 g tagliatelle pasta
125 g piece of Parmesan cheese, flaked.

1 Flatten capsicums by pressing gently with hand. Place under hot grill and cook until skin blisters and becomes black. Remove capsicums and place inside a plastic bag. Leave until cool enough to handle.
2 Cook pork sausage gently until crisp. Remove and drain on absorbent paper. Remove excess fat from pan. Add butter, allow to melt, add onion and cook until golden brown and soft. Add wine, stock, tomato paste, sugar and pepper. Cook on medium heat, uncovered, until sauce has reduced by half.
3 Cook pasta in large quantity of boiling water. While pasta is cooking, remove skin from peppers and cut into thin strips.
4 Combine sauce, sausage and prepared capsicum. Pour mixture over cooked, drained pasta. Toss gently. Top with flaked Parmesan cheese.
Note: To flake Parmesan cheese, run potato peeler over flat edge of cheese to produce one fine flake of cheese.

Fresh Artichoke Omelette

A member of the thistle family, the perfect artichoke is heavy for its size, with stiff leaves. Try this combination of egg and artichoke with a touch of lemon.

PREPARATION TIME: *15 minutes + 15 minutes soaking*
COOKING TIME: *15 minutes*
SERVES 4–6

6 small globe artichokes
3 tablespoons lemon juice

3 cups iced water
¼ cup olive oil
1 clove garlic, slivered
8 large eggs
pepper, to taste
¼ cup chopped Italian parsley
lemon wedges for garnish

1 Wash artichokes, pull away any coarse outer leaves. Cut one third of the top off each artichoke. Trim stems. Slice 'flowers' thinly from top down through the stem. Soak for 15 minutes in combined lemon juice and water. Drain, pat dry.

2 Heat oil in large frying pan, add garlic slivers and cook gently 1–2 minutes. Add artichokes and cook slowly until they are pale golden brown, about 10 minutes.

3 Beat eggs until well combined; add pepper and parsley. Pour eggs over artichokes and continue cooking until eggs are set, lifting edges of omelette with a spatula to let uncooked egg run underneath.

4 Cut into wedges to serve. Garnish with lemon wedges.

Note: To save time, canned artichokes can be used. Simply drain and fry for 3–4 minutes until golden brown.

Persian Baked Eggs and Fresh Artichoke Omelette

If potatoes have a green spot they can be peeled deeply before cooking and they will be quite safe to eat. Potatoes greened all over their surface should not be eaten at all, as this deep greening indicates a concentration of solanine which can be mildy toxic. Avoid buying any potatoes that show any signs of greening and take care to store potatoes in a cool dark airy place.

Carrot Parsnip Omelette

The combination of carrot and parsnip gives a special flavour to this basic omelette recipe.

PREPARATION TIME: *10 minutes*
COOKING TIME: *12–15 minutes*
SERVES *2–4*

60 g butter
1 clove garlic, crushed
2 parsnips, peeled and grated
2 carrots, peeled and grated
3 tablespoons chopped Italian parsley
4 eggs
freshly ground black pepper
2 teaspoons olive oil

1 Melt butter, add garlic and fry 1 minute without browning. Add parsnip and carrot and cook gently with lid on pan for 10 minutes. Allow to cool.
2 Beat eggs just enough to combine. Add parsley and freshly ground black pepper and stir in cooled parsnip and carrot.
3 Heat oil in omelette or small pan. Pour in mixture to cover base of pan. Lift edges of omelette with spatula to allow uncooked egg to run underneath.
4 When omelette is set on top, turn over or brown under hot grill. Serve warm with crisp green salad.

Carrot Pilaf

The addition of golden syrup, which gives a sweet caramel flavour to the rice, betrays the Turkish inspiration of this recipe: the Turkish sweet tooth is legendary. Pilaf is considered to be the King of Dishes — try this variation and you'll be sure to agree.

PREPARATION TIME: *15 minutes*
COOKING TIME: *25 minutes*
SERVES *4–6*

2 cups long-grain rice
2 tablespoons butter
2 tablespoons olive oil
2 cups coarsely grated carrots
finely ground black pepper
1 tablespoon golden syrup

2½ cups chicken stock
1 cup white wine
½ cup chopped pistachios

1 Wash rice until water runs clear. Drain well.
2 Heat butter and oil in heavy-based pan. Add rice; fry 3–4 minutes. Add carrot and pepper; fry for 5 minutes, stirring constantly. Add golden syrup and mix thoroughly.
3 Add stock and wine. Bring to the boil, reduce heat to low, cover with tight-fitting lid and cook for 20–25 minutes or until rice is tender.
4 Place in serving bowl. Sprinkle over pistachios.
Note: Rice must be washed well under cold running water when preparing a pilaf, to ensure light fluffy rice grains.

Eggs with Potatoes

This dish is Lyonnaise in origin. The French are renowned for their potato dishes. Try serving it as a supper or luncheon dish served with a tossed salad. As an accompaniment it marries well with lightly grilled chicken or seafood.

PREPARATION TIME: *40 minutes*
COOKING TIME: *30–40 minutes*
SERVES *4–6*

1 kg baby potatoes
8 hard-boiled eggs, halved
125 g butter
1 cup chopped spring onions
freshly ground pepper
½ cup chopped parsley
¼ cup tarragon wine vinegar

1 Bring a large saucepan of water to the boil and cook potatoes in water until they are just tender; cool. Arrange in a well greased casserole dish. Scatter eggs over the potatoes.
2 Melt butter in a saucepan and cook until golden brown, add spring onions and toss quickly, and then add pepper, parsley and wine vinegar. Pour over potato and egg mixture. Cover with lid or buttered foil.
3 Place in oven at 180°C to heat through gently, about 10 minutes.
Note: Do not overcook or eggs will toughen.

Eggs with Potatoes, Carrot Pilaf and Carrot Parsnip Omelette

31

CHEESE AND YOGHURT

Home-made fresh cheeses and yoghurt are delightful additions to your larder and they're surprisingly simple to make. Fresh soft cottage-style cheese can be served with salad, fruit salad and jacket potatoes, or you can add herbs and serve with Middle Eastern flat breads.

Yoghurt also is easy to make. Use fresh home-made yoghurt to marinate meats and poultry and enrich casseroles, stews and hot vegetable dishes. With a little effort yoghurt can be made into small soft cheeses: rolled in herbs and paprika they will keep well in olive oil.

With a little patience and practice cheese and yoghurt making will become an extremely easy and enjoyable task.

Soft Cheese with Herbs

PREPARATION TIME: *30 minutes + 24 hours standing*
COOKING TIME: *nil*
MAKES 250 g

250 g cottage cheese
½ cup sour cream
2 teaspoons chopped chives
2 teaspoons chopped parsley
2 cloves garlic, crushed
salt
freshly ground black pepper

1 Press cottage cheese and sour cream through fine sieve until smooth.
2 Gradually beat the chopped chives and parsley and crushed garlic into the cheese mixture. Add salt and freshly ground black pepper to taste.
3 Pack the mixture into muslin-lined sieve or draining mould. Fold muslin over cheese, place a small weight on top and refrigerate for at least 24 hours.
4 Unmould cheese and serve with salad greens, capers and melba toast.

1 Press cottage cheese and sour cream through a fine sieve until smooth. Beat in herbs, garlic and seasonings.

2 Pack the mixture into a muslin-lined sieve or draining mould and fold the muslin over the cheese.

Crème Fraîche

Crème Fraîche is the rich, slightly tart cream used to dress fresh seasonal fruits, savoury dishes and vegetables.

PREPARATION TIME: *10 minutes + 24 hours standing*
COOKING TIME: *nil*
MAKES 2 cups

250 mL cream
250 mL sour cream

1 Combine cream and sour cream in bowl, cover and stand at room temperature until cream has thickened. This can take up to 1 or 2 days, depending on the ambient temperature.
2 When thickened, cover and refrigerate before using. Crème Fraîche will keep for up to one week, covered in the refrigerator.

Home-Made Yoghurt

Although plain yoghurt is available commercially, it can be very easily prepared at home. This recipe produces a very thick, creamy yoghurt.

PREPARATION TIME: *6 hours +*
2–3 hours chilling
COOKING TIME: *20 minutes*
MAKES *2 cups*

3 cups full-cream milk
⅓ cup full-cream milk powder
⅓ cup plain yoghurt

1 Set aside ¼ cup of milk. Combine rest with milk powder in saucepan and heat gently to boiling point until froth rises. Reduce heat and allow milk to simmer very gently for 20 minutes.
2 Allow milk to cool to lukewarm (blood heat). Test with thermometer: it should be 45°C. Alternatively you can put your little finger in the milk: you should be just able to feel the heat. Remove skin from top and very gently stir in yoghurt combined with ¼ cup milk.
3 Pour into sterilised jars. Seal. Place jars in boiler or saucepan, fill with hot water from tap. Wrap in blanket to keep warm. Wait at least 6 hours before disturbing. Chill well 3–4 hours before using.

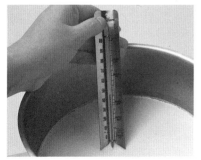

Milk must cool to 45°C before adding starter yoghurt.

1 To make Labana, first combine yoghurt and salt and mix well in a bowl.

2 Line a fine sieve with damp muslin, pour in yoghurt and stand sieve over a large bowl.

3 When cheese is firm, take small pieces and roll into balls. Roll cheese balls in paprika or herbs.

Labana

Labana are soft small cheese balls made from yoghurt, rolled in herbs and paprika and stored in olive oil. They can be served as part of an antipasto plate or with olives and flat breads. If you prefer, fresh labana can be rolled and served with honey and cinnamon as a delightful dessert.

PREPARATION TIME: *30 minutes*
+ 24 hours standing
COOKING TIME: *nil*
MAKES *300 g*

500 mL yoghurt
1 teaspoon salt
paprika
dried or fresh herbs, finely chopped

1 Combine yoghurt and salt; mix well. Line a fine sieve with damp muslin and pour yoghurt into sieve. Stand sieve over a large bowl and refrigerate overnight.
2 The whey from the cheese will drain away. You will need to let the cheese drain until it is quite firm, which can take up to two days.
3 When cheese is quite firm, roll into small balls. Roll the cheese balls over paprika and herbs. Carefully place in a large jar and cover with olive oil.

Poultry & Game

CHICKEN, DUCK, RABBIT AND SMALL GAME are popular main dish ingredients in country food everywhere. You'll find some tasty examples of them in this special collection. In Peru, they team chicken with chillies; in Hungary they cook it with paprika; in China they steam it with ginger; in France, they accompany chicken with prunes, duck with olives and rabbit with mustard. The traditional provincial casseroles, fricassées and pies in this chapter come from many lands. They're inexpensive, straightforward and guaranteed to transform everyday meals into country-style feasts and celebrations.

Country Chicken, Quails with Tarragon and Pancetta (page 36) served with Polenta (page 83) and Sherried Duck with Olives and Walnuts (page 36)

Sherried Duck with Olives and Walnuts

A Spanish-inspired dish, this duck braised in combined sherry and stock is tasty and tender. If you prefer a crisp skin, uncover the bird for the last 15 minutes of cooking.

PREPARATION TIME: *20 minutes*
COOKING TIME: *1 hour 35 minutes*
SERVES 4–6

2 tablespoons olive oil
1 × 2 kg duck, cleaned and trussed
2 onions, halved
2 carrots, cut into large pieces
¼ cup medium dry sherry
¼ cup chicken stock or water
40g butter
2 tablespoons flour
¼ cup medium dry sherry extra
½ cup fresh orange juice
½ cup chicken stock or water extra
½ cup stuffed green olives, warmed in brine
½ cup walnut halves, warmed in oven

Duck is the poultry most prized by gourmets. Though not very meaty, what there is makes delectable eating. Before cooking a whole duck remove all the excess fat and press the oil glands near the base of the tail to empty them. If desired rub a little salt into the skin for added crispness. If in doubt as to the tenderness of the bird braise it slowly, basting well.

1 Heat olive oil in large baking dish on top of stove. Add duck, onion and carrots. Gently turn duck to brown all over, being careful not to split the skin. Pour over combined dry sherry and stock or water. Cover with aluminium foil. Place in oven at 180°C for 1 hour. Baste occasionally with juices during cooking.
2 Remove duck and vegetables from baking dish. Reserve any remaining liquid. Discard vegetables.
3 Place baking dish on top of stove over medium heat, add butter to pan and allow to melt and brown, scraping pan; do not allow butter to burn. Remove pan from heat, stir in flour. Gradually add combined extra sherry, orange juice, extra stock and any reserve liquid. Return to heat and cook, stirring constantly, until mixture boils and thickens.
4 Put duck back in pan and spoon over sauce. Cover and bake at 180°C for 15–20 minutes or until duck is tender. Place duck on heated serving dish, pour over sauce. Garnish with warm stuffed olives and walnut halves.

Quails with Tarragon and Pancetta

Quails are the smallest of the game birds; they can be ordered through poultry shops. We recommend two per person.

PREPARATION TIME: *20 minutes*
COOKING TIME: *40 minutes*
SERVES *4*

8 small quails
½ cup plain flour
¼ cup olive oil
2 onions, diced
300 g button mushrooms
100 g pancetta
1½ cups red wine
½ cup chicken stock
1 tablespoon redcurrant jelly
pepper to taste
1 teaspoon tarragon leaves

1 Tie quails into neat shapes. Toss in flour. Heat oil in a heavy-based pan and cook quails, turning to brown on all sides. Remove from pan.
2 Add onion to pan and cook 1 minute. Add mushrooms and pancetta; cook until mushrooms soften. Add wine and chicken stock and stir until mixture comes to the boil. Add redcurrant jelly, pepper and tarragon.
3 Return quails to sauce and simmer gently, turning quails from time to time until they are tender and sauce has thickened, about 20–30 minutes.
4 Serve quails on a warm serving plate with Polenta (page 83) and vegetables in season.

Country Chicken

This country favourite is from Tuscany, Italy. Slow casseroling of the chicken develops the flavours and reduces the stock so that the sauce thickens. This dish can be made in advance as it reheats well.

PREPARATION TIME: *40 minutes*
COOKING TIME: *60 minutes*
SERVES 6

1 kg chicken thigh fillets, skin removed
⅓ cup flour
2 medium leeks
1 x 400 g can tomatoes
300 g button mushrooms
60 g butter
¼ cup olive oil
2 cloves garlic, crushed
1 cup dry white wine
1 teaspoon sugar
½ teaspoon ground black pepper

1 Remove fat from chicken pieces and toss in flour. Wash and thinly slice leeks. Drain tomatoes, reserving juice, and chop flesh. Wipe mushrooms over and halve.
2 Heat half the butter and olive oil in a heavy pan. When hot, add the chicken pieces a few at a time and fry until golden both sides. Remove chicken and put into a casserole.
3 Add remaining oil and butter to the pan, cook garlic 1 minute, add leeks, cook 3 minutes, then add halved mushrooms and fry 2 minutes. Remove all ingredients from pan and scatter over chicken.
4 Pour wine into pan and reduce to about ¼ cup. Add chopped tomatoes and juice plus sugar and pepper; simmer gently 10 minutes. Pour over chicken and vegetables in casserole dish.
5 Cover casserole dish with lid and cook in oven at 160°C for 40 minutes or until chicken is cooked. Serve with fried Polenta (page 83) and seasonal salad vegetables.

Chicken Paprika with Caraway Dumplings

Paprika can be hot or sweet and earthy in flavour. The best paprika comes from Hungary, where it is used in the well-known dish, Goulash.

PREPARATION TIME: 25 minutes
COOKING TIME: 50 minutes
SERVES 6

1 tablespoon olive oil
1 tablespoon butter
2 onions, chopped
1 kg chicken thigh fillets, cut in half
1 large tomato, peeled and chopped
2 tablespoons tomato paste
1 tablespoon sweet paprika

1 tablespoon brown sugar
1 tablespoon brown vinegar
1 cup chicken stock
2 tablespoons flour
½ cup sour cream
DUMPLINGS
2 cups self-raising flour
60 g butter
1 teaspoon caraway seeds
½ cup water
½ cup milk
beaten egg for glaze

1 Heat oil and butter in large frying pan. Add onion and cook until soft and golden brown. Add chicken and cook until well browned all over.
2 Stir in tomato, tomato paste, stock, paprika, brown sugar and vinegar. Place lid on pan and cook until chicken is tender, about 30 minutes.
3 Remove chicken from pan and place in casserole. Combine flour and sour cream. Gradually add cream mixture to simmering liquid, stirring constantly until mixture boils and thickens. Pour sauce over chicken and place in oven at 180°C to keep hot.
4 To prepare dumplings, sift flour into basin, rub in butter and add caraway seeds. Make a well in centre, add combined milk and water and mix to form a soft dough. Place spoonfuls of mixture on top of hot chicken and glaze with beaten egg. Place lid on casserole. Bake at 180°C for 8–10 minutes. Remove lid and cook until dumplings are golden brown, about 5 minutes.
Note: If preferred, dumplings can be cooked in a pot of simmering water. It will result in a soft, moist dumpling.

Chicken Paprika with Caraway Dumplings

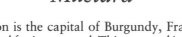

Rabbit with Dijon Mustard

Dijon is the capital of Burgundy, France, famed for its mustard. This mustard is very mild, but aromatic.

PREPARATION TIME: *35 minutes*
COOKING TIME: *1½ hours*
SERVES 6

2 rabbits (about 1 kg each)
¼ cup flour
freshly ground pepper
½ teaspoon dry mustard
60 g butter
2 cloves garlic, crushed
250 g small mushrooms
1 tablespoon olive oil
3 rashers bacon, rind removed, chopped
2 onions, chopped
2 carrots, diced
1 parsnip, diced
1 cup white wine
½ cup chicken stock
6 whole allspice
1½ tablespoons Dijon mustard
2 tablespoons parsley
2 tablespoons cream

1 Clean rabbits and cut each into 6 portions. Put flour, pepper and dry mustard in a plastic bag and add rabbit pieces a few at a time. Toss well to coat with seasoned flour.
2 Heat butter in pan and add garlic, stirring 1 minute. Add rabbit pieces and cook until well browned on both sides; remove. Add whole mushrooms to pan, cook 1 minute and remove. Add oil to pan and then bacon, onion, carrot and parsnip. Cook, stirring, for 3 minutes.
3 Place rabbit in large ovenproof dish and add cooked vegetables, wine, stock, allspice and mustard. Cover and cook in a moderate oven for about 1½ hours or until rabbit is tender. Stir in parsley and cream and serve immediately.

Game Pie

The word 'game' refers to wild birds and animals that are hunted for sport or food. Today many game farms are breeding game for the commercial market.

PREPARATION TIME: *35 minutes*
COOKING TIME: *45 minutes*
SERVES 6–8

1kg boneless game meat (hare fillets,
boned pheasant or venison)
30 g dried mushrooms, soaked in water
for 10 minutes
60 g butter
3 rashers bacon, rind removed,
diced
2 large onions, chopped
3 tablespoons flour
½ teaspoon dried mustard
¼ cup port
½ cup red wine
6 juniper berries
1 cup chicken or beef stock
½ tablespoon fresh thyme leaves
¼ cup chopped parsley
pepper
1 x 375 g pkt puff pastry
egg glaze

1 Cut game into 2 cm pieces, heat butter and fry meat quickly to brown; remove from pan. Add bacon to remaining oil in pan, cook until crisp, remove. Add sliced onions and fry until golden. Sprinkle flour over onions and allow to brown.
2 Stir through mustard, port, red wine, berries, stock, mushrooms and thyme leaves. Continue stirring until mixture comes to boil. Add game and simmer gently until game is tender, about 30–40 minutes. Preheat oven to 210°C.
3 Ladle meat into a greased casserole. Cook sauce until it thickens. Season with pepper. Pour over meat and sprinkle with parsley.
4 Roll out pastry to fit casserole dish. Glaze edge of dish and cover casserole with pastry lid. Glaze lid and slit to allow steam to escape. Cook in preheated oven until pastry browns and filling warms through.
Note: Do not overcook, as it will make the game meat tough.

Game can be placed in two categories: firstly feathered game, which includes quail, pheasant, wild duck, guinea fowl and pigeon; and secondly furred game, which includes rabbit, hare and venison. Young game can be roasted, but older game will be slightly tougher and is best suited to the long slow cooking of casseroles or stews. Marinating also tenderises and flavours game meats.

Game Pie and Rabbit with Dijon Mustard

Left: Steamed Chicken with Ginger; right: Two-In-One Chicken

Steamed Chicken with Ginger

A whole chicken is used in this Asian-style steamed chicken, but any chicken pieces can be substituted. Chicken is delicious served cold as part of a picnic hamper.

PREPARATION TIME: *20 minutes*
COOKING TIME: *25 minutes*
SERVES 6

1 x 1.5 kg chicken
1 tablespoon grated fresh ginger
2 tablespoons light soy sauce
2 tablespoons dry sherry
1 tablespoon honey
½ teaspoon sesame oil
2 tablespoons toasted sesame seeds
2 spring onions, shredded

1 Cut chicken into bite-sized pieces. Wipe with paper towel. Place on heatproof plate.
2 Combine ginger, soy sauce, sherry, honey and sesame oil. Pour over chicken, making sure all pieces are well coated.
3 Place plate in steamer or container of boiling water. Cover steamer with lid or greased aluminium foil. Steam on high heat for 25 minutes or until chicken is tender and cooked through.
4 Place on serving plate. Sprinkle with sesame seeds and spring onion.

Coriander and Lemon Chicken

Coriander is sometimes referred to as 'Chinese parsley'. It does not take well to long cookery, so it is best added to dishes with a relatively short cooking time, or added towards the end of the cooking time.

PREPARATION TIME: *15 minutes*
COOKING TIME: *20 minutes*
SERVES 6

For easy grating of ginger, peel and store in container in freezer. When required, bring straight from freezer, grate and return unused portion to freezer.

 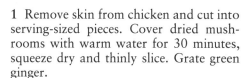
1 kg boned chicken breasts
¼ cup olive oil
2 teaspoons grated ginger
2 cloves garlic, crushed
2 onions, chopped finely
1 cup chicken stock
¾ cup chopped coriander
2 tablespoons chopped chives
¼ cup chopped parsley
⅓ cup lemon juice
2 teaspoons cornflour
1 tablespoon water

1 Skin chicken breasts and cut in halves. Heat oil in pan, cook chicken breasts quickly and remove. Add ginger, garlic and onions to remaining oil in pan and fry stirring for 2 minutes.

2 Return chicken to the pan with stock, coriander, chives, parsley and lemon juice. Simmer chicken in sauce 15 minutes. Remove chicken fillets with a slotted spoon and place on serving plate. Keep warm.

3 Blend cornflour and water, add to sauce and stir till sauce thickens. Pour over chicken fillets.

Two-In-One Chicken

The chicken is cooked with flavouring liquid to produce a tasty soup. The chicken is removed and served separately with a dipping sauce.

PREPARATION TIME: *15 minutes*
COOKING TIME: *40 minutes*
SERVES 6

1 x 1.5 kg chicken
3 cups chicken stock
6 large dried Chinese mushrooms
2 cm piece green ginger, peeled
⅔ cup chopped spring onions
2 small cucumbers, peeled, seeded, chopped
½ cup chopped coriander
¼ cup dry sherry
1 tablespoon dark soy sauce
1 tablespoon sesame oil
1 x 400 g can straw mushrooms, drained
DIPPING SAUCE
2 tablespoons light soy sauce
2 tablespoons sherry
2 tablespoons roasted sesame seeds
½ teaspoons chilli sauce
few drops sesame oil
¼ teaspoon grated ginger

1 Remove skin from chicken and cut into serving-sized pieces. Cover dried mushrooms with warm water for 30 minutes, squeeze dry and thinly slice. Grate green ginger.

2 Place chicken in a large saucepan and add stock, ginger, spring onions, cucumbers and coriander. Simmer gently until chicken is tender, about 40 minutes.

3 Add sherry, soy sauce, sesame oil, straw mushrooms and soaked mushrooms. Heat through. Lift out chicken pieces, serve soup.

4 Combine all ingredients for Dipping Sauce and serve with chicken pieces and boiled rice.

Sardinian Rabbit Stew

Sardinian Rabbit Stew

Saffron is an important flavouring in Sardinian cuisine. Choose small fresh rabbits, as they have a milder flavour and are very tender. This dish is excellent served cold the day after making.

PREPARATION TIME: *20 minutes*
COOKING TIME: *45 minutes*
SERVES 4–6

2 small rabbits cut into serving-sized
pieces
1 cup plain flour
1 teaspoon powdered saffron
pepper
¼ cup olive oil
1 onion, finely chopped
2 cloves garlic, crushed
¼ cup capers, drained and chopped
⅓ cup dry white wine
¼ cup white wine vinegar
⅓ cup chicken stock or water

1 Wash and dry rabbit. Combine flour, saffron and pepper and coat rabbit in seasoned flour.

2 Heat oil in large pan. Add rabbit in single layer and cook until well browned all over. Remove rabbit and wipe excess oil from pan.

3 Add onion and garlic to pan and cook until soft and golden brown. Add capers, wine, vinegar and stock. Bring to the boil, reduce heat and simmer for 5 minutes.

3 Return rabbit to pan. Cook covered for 40–45 minutes or until rabbit is tender.

4 Serve hot or cold with vegetables or a fresh green salad.

Coriander is pungent and lively with a unique scent. Also known as Chinese parsley, it belongs to the same family as parsley, caraway, dill and fennel. Use coriander to flavour chicken, lamb and vegetable dishes. Asian style stir-fry dishes and salads are also enhanced by this zesty herb.

Chicken and Creamy Chilli Sauce

If fresh chillies are unavailable, use whole dried chillies soaked for 30 minutes in lukewarm water. Drain and prepare as required.

An excellent dish for the buffet table — boneless chicken covered in a creamy bread-thickened sauce with a hint of chilli. A combination of eggs, olives and chillies used as garnish results in an eye-catching presentation suitable for entertaining.

PREPARATION TIME: *40 minutes*
COOKING TIME: *20 minutes*
SERVES 4

Coriander and Lemon Chicken (page 40)

8 *slices fresh white bread, crusts removed*
1 *cup milk*
1 *tablespoon olive oil*
1 *onion, finely chopped*
2 *cloves garlic, crushed*
¼–½ *teaspoon chilli powder*
200 g *ground almonds*
freshly ground black pepper
1 *cup cream*
4 *chicken breast fillets, cooked and thinly sliced*
3 *hard-boiled eggs, quartered*
12 *large black olives*
1 *fresh red chilli, cut into fine strips*

1 Soak bread in milk for 5 minutes. Squeeze to make a thick paste.
2 Heat oil in pan, add onion and garlic, cook until soft but do not brown. Add bread and milk paste, chilli powder, almonds and pepper; mix thoroughly. Simmer, stirring, for 5 minutes.
3 Stir in cream, add chicken and cook on low heat until chicken is heated through.
4 Place chicken mixture in heated serving dish. Arrange eggs, olives and chilli strips on top in decorative pattern. Serve accompanied by green salad.

Casserole of Chicken and Pork with Fruit

This casserole is a medley of meats, fruits and flavours which results in tender chicken and pork in a sweet, spicy sauce.

PREPARATION TIME: *25 minutes*
COOKING TIME: *40 minutes*
SERVES 4–6

¼ *cup olive oil*
4 *half chicken breast fillets, cut in half*
3 *pork medallions, cut in half*
2 *cups chicken stock*
¾ *cup whole almonds, toasted*
2 *tablespoons sesame seeds, toasted*
1 *fresh red chilli, chopped*
2 *tomatoes, peeled, seeded and chopped*
1 *teaspoon cinnamon*
¼ *cup sweet vermouth*
2 *large apples, peeled, cored and cut into thick slices*
6 *slices fresh pineapple, cored and cut into quarters*
6 *large fresh apricots, cut in half and stoned*

1 Heat oil in large pan. Add chicken and pork. Cook until well browned.

3 Pour mixture over chicken and pork, add vermouth, cover and cook over low heat for 25 minutes. Add apple, pineapple and apricots and simmer for 15 minutes longer or until fruit is tender and meats are cooked.
4 Serve with boiled white rice.

Braised Chicken with Prunes

The French often cook poultry with fruit. This recipe combines apples, cognac and prunes to produce a unique flavour.

PREPARATION TIME: *15 minutes + 24 hours marinating*
COOKING TIME: *50 minutes*
SERVES 6

1 x 1.5 kg *chicken*
⅔ *cup apple sauce*
3 *tablespoons cognac or brandy*
⅓ *cup red wine vinegar*
1 *cup dry white wine*
2 *bay leaves*
1 *teaspoon peppercorns*
1 *teaspoon thyme leaves*
4 *whole cloves garlic*
1 *leek, finely chopped*
½ *cup flour*
pepper

¼ cup olive oil
1 cup pitted prunes

1 Cut chicken into serving-sized portions. Combine apple sauce, cognac, vinegar, wine, bay leaves, peppercorns, thyme, garlic and leek and mix well. Add chicken pieces, cover and place in refrigerator for 24 hours. Turn chicken pieces in the marinade occasionally.

2 Drain chicken well, reserving the marinade. Season flour and lightly toss chicken pieces in flour to coat. Heat oil in a large pan. Cook chicken pieces, browning well on all sides.

3 Strain marinade and add liquid to chicken in the pan with prunes. Simmer gently uncovered, turning chicken pieces occasionally for about 40 minutes or until chicken is tender and sauce thickens. Serve with vegetables in season and garnish with leek shreds.

Casserole of Chicken and Pork with Fruit and Braised Chicken with Prunes

Meat Stews, Braises & Roasts

L AMB, PORK, BEEF AND VEAL have inspired an amazing variety of cookery techniques and recipes for centuries. Country meat cuisine is simple and sustaining, combining less expensive cuts with tenderising flavouring ingredients and produce from the vegetable plot or orchard. We present some delectable examples from France, Italy, the Middle East, England and America. Fruit is joined with pork, while veal tastes superb with potatoes and zucchini. Meatballs go with eggplant and lamb with potatoes — we urge you to try them all. You'll love them.

Lamb and Vegetable Ragoût and Corned Beef with Peach and Ginger (page 46)

Corned Beef with Peach and Ginger

America has a cuisine as varied as its population. This recipe no doubt started out as corned beef and cabbage but has evolved into beef baked with fresh fruit flavoured with marmalade and topped with shredded coconut — a touch of the tropics, perhaps.

PREPARATION TIME: *20 minutes*
COOKING TIME: *1½ hours*
SERVES 4–6

1.5 kg piece corned silverside
1 orange, quartered
1 onion, quartered
4–6 small apples, cored and halved
½ cup chopped peaches, fresh or canned
⅓ cup lime marmalade
1 tablespoon chopped glacé ginger
½ cup shredded coconut

1 Place corned silverside, orange and onion in large saucepan and cover with water. Put lid on pan, bring to the boil, reduce heat to simmer and cook for 1¼ hours or until tender when tested with a skewer. Remove meat from cooking liquid and put into ovenproof dish.
2 Place prepared apples, cavity side up, around meat. Combine peaches, marmalade, ginger and coconut. Spoon on top of meat and into each apple cavity.
3 Bake at 180°C for 15 minutes. Serve thickly sliced with apple.

1 tablespoon oil
30 g butter
1.25 kg lamb fillets, cut into 3 cm cubes
2 cloves garlic, crushed
10 whole baby onions, peeled
10 whole baby carrots, peeled
10 whole baby new potatoes, peeled
3 parsnips, cut into 5 cm strips
⅓ cup flour
4 cups chicken stock
1 cup white wine
2 teaspoons French mustard
1 tablespoon Worcestershire sauce
250 g small green beans, topped and tailed
125 g whole baby sugar peas
freshly ground pepper
½ teaspoon dried rosemary

1 Heat oil and butter in large pan, add lamb in single layer and cook until well browned all over. Remove, add garlic, onions, carrots, potatoes and parsnips and cook until well browned all over. Remove vegetables from pan.
2 Add flour to pan and cook, stirring, for 1 minute. Remove from heat, gradually stir in stock and wine. Add mustard and Worcestershire sauce. Return to heat, stirring constantly until mixture boils and thickens. Return lamb, onions, carrots, potatoes and parsnip to sauce and add pepper and rosemary. Cover pan and cook for 45 minutes or until meat and vegetables are tender.
3 Add beans and sugar peas and cook for further 10 minutes.

Note: Ragoût can be frozen for up to 3 months. Thaw in refrigerator before reheating.

Lancashire Hotpot was created in the industrial north of England. Factory workers would prepare this casserole of mutton or lamb, oysters, mushrooms and potatoes, place it in a special earthenware pot and leave it to cook slowly in the oven while they laboured in factories and cotton mills.

Lamb and Oyster Casserole

Lamb and Vegetable Ragoût

Ragoût is the French term for meat and vegetables cooked in a simmering liquid. In this case it is lamb and selected vegetables cooked in water and wine, with added flavourings. By choosing lamb fillet the cooking time is reduced. Any boneless cut of lamb can be used — adjust cooking time to suit choice of meat.

PREPARATION TIME: *45 minutes*
COOKING TIME: *55 minutes*
SERVES 4–6

Lamb and Oyster Casserole

This dish resembles the traditional Lancashire hotpot. When oysters were plentiful they were added to the basic lamb stew. Try this updated version with the extra flavour of smoked oysters.

PREPARATION TIME: *25 minutes*
COOKING TIME: *1 hour 45 minutes*
SERVES 4

1.25 kg lamb neck chops, fat removed
4 large onions, sliced

1 kg potatoes, peeled and thickly sliced
1 jar smoked oysters
freshly ground black pepper
2 cups chicken stock
½ cup white wine
1 tablespoon fresh rosemary, chopped
1 tablespoon butter

1 Place layer of chops in greased oven-proof dish. Cover with layer of onions, potatoes and oysters, seasoning each layer with black pepper. Repeat layers, ending with potatoes.
2 Combine stock, wine and rosemary, pour over and dot top with butter. Cover and bake at 180°C for 1–1½ hours.
3 Remove lid and cook further 15–20 minutes or until top is golden brown.
4 Serve straight from ovenproof dish, accompanied by steamed green vegetables.

Lamb Shanks with Garlic

The meat on lamb shanks is very sweet. This delicious casserole can be prepared ahead of time and reheated. Lamb neck chops can be substituted if shanks are not available.

PREPARATION TIME: *15 minutes*
COOKING TIME: *1¼ hours*
SERVES 4

¼ cup olive oil
8 lamb shanks
10 cloves garlic, peeled
½ cup white wine
1 leek, finely sliced
2 medium carrots, chopped
2 teaspoons rosemary leaves
1½ cups chicken stock
2 teaspoons cornflour

1 Heat oil in a heavy-based pan with a tight fitting lid. Cook shanks on all sides until well browned. Add whole garlic, cover pan, reduce heat to low and simmer gently 45 minutes. (During this time the shanks will cook in their own juices.)
2 Remove garlic and add wine, leeks, carrots and rosemary. Cover and simmer a further 30 minutes. Remove meat and vegetables with a slotted spoon and transfer to a serving plate. Keep warm.
3 Blend cornflour with a little cold water and add with stock to pan juices. Bring to the boil and cook until thickened. Pour over meat and vegetables. Serve with mashed potatoes.

Garlic has a long history. An ancient belief was that it gave strength and courage. It is recorded that the labourers who built the Pyramids were given garlic for strength and nourishment. In the Middle Ages garlic was also used to ward off the evils of witches and demons. It was and to some extent still is prized for its medicinal use in the treatment of coughs, colds and poor digestion.

Lamb Shanks with Garlic

Tasty Oxtail Stew

This is a two-course meal cooked in one pot. The cooking stock becomes a savoury meat broth topped with toasted bread and cheese. The meat and vegetables are served on a platter, moistened with a little of the stock as a gravy.

PREPARATION TIME: *55 minutes*
COOKING TIME: *2 hours*
SERVES *4*

2 tablespoons olive oil
1 tablespoon butter
500 g oxtail cut into 4 cm sections
500 g beef spare ribs, cut into 4 cm sections
500 g lamb forequarter chops, cut into 4 cm pieces
6 small carrots, peeled, left whole
6 small turnips, peeled, cut in half
6 small whole potatoes
4 stalks celery, cut into 4 cm pieces
½ small cabbage, cut into 3 sections
1 ham hock, cut into 5 cm sections
5 cups beef stock
1 onion, studded with 4 cloves
1 bouquet garni consisting of 2 bay leaves, sprig of thyme and parsley
5 juniper berries
5 black peppercorns
1 French bread stick, cut into rounds and toasted
1 cup grated Gruyère cheese

Rich in gelatin and flavour, oxtails are best used in casseroles or soups with long slow cooking time. When buying oxtail look for deep red meat with an equal proportion of meat to bone. The fat should be creamy white in colour.

1 Heat oil and butter in large pan. Add meats and cook over low heat until well browned. Remove and set aside.
2 Add carrots, turnips and whole potatoes to the pan; cook gently until well browned all over.
3 Return meat to pan, add celery, cabbage and ham hock. Pour over beef stock and add onion, bouquet garni, juniper berries and peppercorns. Bring mixture to the boil; reduce heat. Cover and simmer over low heat for 2 hours until meat and vegetables are tender.
4 Remove meat and ham hock to heated serving platter and surround with vegetables. Strain stock and spoon 4 tablespoons of stock over meat and vegetables.
5 Place remaining meat broth in soup tureen. Top toasted bread rounds with cheese and grill until cheese is melted. Place on top of meat broth. Serve meat broth either with or before the platter of meat and vegetables.

Meatballs in Eggplant Sauce

Eggplants or aubergines, as they are also known, are a vegetable found extensively in the Middle Eastern countries. The name eggplant is derived from their distinctive egg shape. They have a smooth, glossy, purple to black skin that should be free from any blemishes. Choose small, firm eggplants with a fresh, green calyx.

PREPARATION TIME: *30 minutes + 20 minutes standing*
COOKING TIME: *30 minutes*
SERVES *6*

6 small eggplants, cut in half
1 tablespoon olive oil
3 tablespoons tomato paste
1 tablespoon white wine vinegar
1 teaspoon sugar
1 kg lean minced beef or lamb
1 egg
2 tablespoons flour
3 tablespoons chopped mint
1 teaspoon cinnamon
1 teaspoon ground allspice
freshly ground black pepper
½ cup flour for coating
oil for shallow frying
mint sprigs for garnish

1 Sprinkle eggplant with salt and leave to stand 20 minutes. Rinse in cold water and pat dry. Brush eggplant with oil. Place in baking dish and bake at 180°C until flesh is soft, about 20 minutes. Peel skin away while eggplants are warm. Blend flesh with tomato paste, vinegar and sugar and set aside.
2 Combine minced meat, egg, flour, chopped mint, cinnamon, allspice and black pepper. Using hands, mix and knead mixture until smooth. Using wetted hands, roll into balls and coat in flour.
3 Heat oil in shallow frying pan on gentle heat. Fry half meatballs until golden brown and cooked through. Repeat with remaining meatballs. Drain well on absorbent paper.
4 Remove oil from pan and wipe out with absorbent paper. Pour in puréed eggplant mixture and cook gently for 10 minutes. Add meatballs and cook gently for 5 minutes or until meatballs are heated through. Serve with boiled rice. Garnish with mint.

Tasty Oxtail Stew and Meatballs in Eggplant Sauce

Tripe with Creamy Green Pepper Sauce, Pork Medallions with Pears and Quick Cassoulet

Tripe with Creamy Green Pepper Sauce

Tripe is the lining of the stomach of cattle or sheep. It can either be smooth or honeycomb texture. When tripe is purchased it has been partially cooked, but to ensure tenderness it will require some long, slow cooking in flavoured liquid. It can then be cooked in a variety of ways.

PREPARATION TIME: *1½ hours*
COOKING TIME: *25 minutes*
SERVES 4

500 g tripe
1 L chicken stock
1 onion, quartered
2 bay leaves
few parsley stalks
1 tablespoon olive oil
1 onion, finely chopped
1 tablespoon green peppercorns
1 tablespoon tarragon vinegar
½ cup sour cream blended with 1 teaspoon cornflour

1 Place tripe in saucepan, add chicken stock, onion, bay leaves and parsley stalks.

Bring to the boil, cover and simmer 1–1¼ hours or until tender. Drain tripe and cut into very thin strips.
2 Heat oil in pan, add onion and cook gently 2–3 minutes. Add tripe, place lid on pan and cook slowly for 15 minutes.
3 Remove lid, add peppercorns and vinegar and cook, stirring for 1 minute. Add cream mixture and stir constantly until mixture thickens. Serve with vegetables.

Farmhouse Pot Roast

Pot roasting is the method of cooking foods in a large, heavy-based saucepan by first browning in oil and then adding the vegetables and liquid. Food cooked by this method should be very tender and tasty.

PREPARATION TIME: *15 minutes*
COOKING TIME: *1½ hours*
SERVES 6

1 x 1.5 kg rolled beef roast
3 tablespoons flour
1 teaspoon dry mustard
30 g butter
3 rashers bacon, rind removed, sliced

3 carrots, finely chopped
3 sticks celery, finely chopped
2 cups beer
¼ cup tomato purée
2 tablespoons horseradish
½ teaspoon black pepper

1 Combine flour and mustard and rub over rolled roast. Reserve excess flour.
2 Heat butter in large saucepan and cook meat on all sides until well sealed. Remove and stand. Add bacon, carrots and celery to pan and cook, stirring, until bacon is crisp. Add remaining flour, stirring constantly until well browned.
3 Pour in beer and stir until sauce boils and thickens. Add tomato purée, horseradish and pepper and simmer 2 minutes. Add rolled roast, cover and simmer gently 1¼–1½ hours or until meat is tender.
4 Remove meat, slice and transfer to serving plate. Keep warm. Reduce sauce until thickened and pour over meat to serve.

Pork Medallions with Pears

Although this recipe uses pork, either chicken or veal can be substituted with equal success.

PREPARATION TIME: *15 minutes*
COOKING TIME: *40 minutes*
SERVES 6

6 x 3 cm thick pork medallions
¼ cup plain flour
½ teaspoon dry mustard
ground black pepper
3 firm pears, peeled, cored and quartered
30 g butter
30 mL olive oil
1 cup chopped spring onions
1½ cups dry white wine
½ cup orange juice
2 teaspoons grated orange rind
2 tablespoons redcurrant jelly
1 tablespoon French mustard

1 Combine mustard, black pepper and flour in a plastic bag and toss pork in seasoned flour. Reserve leftover seasoned flour. Peel and quarter the pears.
2 Heat butter and olive oil together until hot, quickly cook pork on either side and

remove from pan.
3 Add spring onions to remaining butter and oil in pan. Add remaining seasoned flour and cook until golden brown. Pour in wine and stir until mixture comes to the boil and thickens. Add orange juice, rind, redcurrant jelly and French mustard. Simmer 15 minutes.
4 Add pork medallions to sauce and simmer gently 15 minutes. Turn pork over, add pear quarters and simmer covered for another 15 minutes or until pears are tender. Serve with vegetables in season.

Quick Cassoulet

Cassoulet is a traditional bean dish which originated in Languedoc, France. In this adaptation of it, we have shortened the cooking time by using processed beans. Serve with crusty French bread and salad.

PREPARATION TIME: *25 minutes*
COOKING TIME: *45 minutes*
SERVES 6

Farmhouse Pot Roast

2 tablespoons olive oil
2 rashers bacon, rind removed, chopped
3 brown onions, chopped
2 cloves garlic, crushed
3 sticks celery, chopped
750 g fresh ripe tomatoes, peeled and chopped
½ cup chopped parsley
2 bay leaves
sprig fresh thyme
1 x 400 g can cooked cannellini beans
1 x 400 g can cooked chick peas
1 x 400 g can borlotti or kidney beans
250 g smoked ham, chopped
½ cup tomato purée

1 Heat oil in a heavy-based pan. Add bacon and cook until golden. Cook onions in remaining oil until golden brown. Add garlic, cook 1 minute and then add celery. Cover and reduce heat; simmer 7 minutes. Preheat oven to 190°C.
2 Add fresh tomatoes, parsley, bay leaves and thyme, cover and simmer 25 minutes. Drain and rinse canned beans. Toss beans through sauce with ham and tomato purée. Transfer to a deep casserole dish. Bake in preheated oven for 45 minutes. Serve immediately.

Braised Beef with Anchovies

This recipe can be made with cheaper cuts of meat like blade or round steak. Increase the cooking time, allowing 1–1½ hours cooking over a gentle heat.

PREPARATION TIME: *30 minutes*
COOKING TIME: *40 minutes*
SERVES 6

1.25 kg rump steak
½ cup plain flour
½ teaspoon dry mustard
½ teaspoon dried thyme
½ teaspoon ground pepper
2 tablespoons olive oil
4 medium onions, thinly sliced
3 cloves garlic, crushed
¼ cup red wine vinegar
2 cups red wine
⅓ cup cognac
4 anchovies, mashed
2 tablespoons capers, rinsed
½ cup Italian parsley, finely chopped

1 Trim meat of all fat and cut into 3 cm strips. Combine flour, mustard, thyme and pepper in a plastic bag and shake well. Add meat strips to the bag and toss to coat lightly in flour.
2 Heat 1 tablespoon olive oil in a large heavy-based pan. Add meat strips a few at a time and cook quickly on both sides, remove and continue with remaining pieces of meat.
3 Add other tablespoon of oil to the pan and cook the onions and garlic until golden. Add vinegar and red wine and reduce over a high heat until one cup of liquid remains. Remove one third of the onions for garnish.
4 Add cognac, mashed anchovies and capers. Simmer the sauce for 3 minutes. Return meat to pan and simmer until meat is just cooked.
5 Remove meat to serving platter and keep warm. Cook sauce to reduce and pour over meat. Sprinkle with chopped parsley and garnish with reserved onion. Serve with Polenta and vegetables in season.

Capers are the flower buds from a native North African bush. They are picked by hand, salted and preserved in vinegar. They are primarily used to add piquant flavour to sauces, mayonnaise and seafood dishes and are also used to garnish the classic Salad Niçoise and smoked salmon.

1 Using a sharp knife, trim excess fat from meat. Cut trimmed meat into 3 cm strips.

2 Add meat strips in small batches to flour mixture in plastic bag. Shake bag lightly to coat meat.

3 Add sliced onions and garlic to pan and cook, stirring until golden. Add red wine and vinegar.

4 Add the cognac, mashed anchovies and capers to pan and simmer sauce uncovered for 3 minutes.

Stuffed Lamb with Apricot and Cinnamon Glaze

A mixture of aromatic herbs, spices and ingredients gives the lamb a distinctive Middle Eastern flavour. Basmati rice is from Pakistan; it is long-grained, with a distinctive flavour. Ghee is clarified butter, available from the supermarket.

PREPARATION TIME: *50 minutes*
COOKING TIME: *1½ hours*
SERVES 6

1½ cups Basmati rice
2 tablespoons ghee
3 spring onions, chopped
250 g lean minced beef
¼ cup chopped coriander
¼ cup pine nuts
½ cup raisins
1 teaspoon cinnamon
1 teaspoon garam masala
2½ cups beef stock or water
1 x 1.5 kg boned leg or shoulder of lamb
1 cup dried apricots, soaked in

1½ cups water
1 tablespoon honey
2 teaspoons cinnamon

1 Place rice in sieve and allow cold water to run through until water runs clear. Melt ghee in pan, add spring onions and cook on gentle heat 2–3 minutes. Add beef and allow to cook until golden brown. Add rice and continue to fry 3–4 minutes. Add coriander, pine nuts, raisins, 1 teaspoon cinnamon and garam masala. Stir to combine. Add stock or water, bring to the boil and allow mixture to boil until nearly all liquid has been absorbed. Reduce to very low heat, place lid on pan and cook until rice is tender, about 10–15 minutes. Allow to cool.
2 Remove excess fat from lamb and wipe with damp towel. Fill cavity with rice mixture and secure lamb with string. Place in baking dish, cover with oiled aluminium foil and bake at 180°C for 1¼ hours or until juices run clear when tested.
3 Place apricots in saucepan with soaking liquid, honey and cinnamon. Simmer, covered, until very tender. Cool slightly. Push through a sieve or blend in electric blender.
4 Remove foil from lamb. Pour over apricot mixture, return to oven and cook at 200°C for 7–10 minutes. Serve lamb in thick slices with vegetables.

Ghee or clarified butter is butter with the milk solids and salts removed so that it can be heated to a high temperature without burning. Ghee is used extensively in Indian and Middle Eastern cookery, giving their dishes a rich and distinctive savour.

Braised Beef with Anchovies and Stuffed Lamb with Apricot and Cinnamon Glaze

Provençal Stuffed Beef and Steak and Kidney Pudding

Steak and Kidney Pudding

A classic English dish, loved by all, a nourishing economical meal suitable for family and friends on cold winter nights. Try adding sliced mushrooms to the meat filling for extra flavour.

PREPARATION TIME: *1½ hours*
COOKING TIME: *2½ hours*
SERVES 4–6

❋ ❋

1 kg chuck steak, cut into 3 cm cubes
2 lamb's kidneys, cored and chopped
2 tablespoons seasoned flour
2 tablespoons butter
1 onion, chopped
1 cup water
2 tablespoons dry sherry
2 teaspoons Worcestershire sauce
¼ teaspoon nutmeg
SUET PASTRY
2 cups self-raising flour
125 g fresh suet, shredded, or package suet
⅓ cup ice-cold water

1 Coat steak and kidney in seasoned flour. Melt butter in pan, add onion and fry gently 2–3 minutes. Add steak and kidney and fry gently until well browned all over. Add water, sherry, Worcestershire sauce and nutmeg. Bring to the boil, reduce heat and simmer, covered, for 1½ hours or until meat is tender. Set aside to cool.
2 Sift flour into bowl. Add suet to flour and stir with a knife to distribute evenly. Make well in centre, pour in water and mix with knife until dough clings together. Place on lightly floured board and knead gently 2–3 minutes.
3 Roll dough out into a circle 30 cm in diameter x 5 mm thick. Cut a quarter section out of the circle and set aside — this portion becomes the top. Line a well greased 4-cup pudding basin with the three-quarter circle, sealing the overlap.
4 Place cold filling in pastry-lined basin, mounding in the centre. Brush dough rim with cold water. Roll out remaining dough to fit and crimp edges together using fingers or fork. Cover with round of double thickness of greased foil or greaseproof paper and secure with string. Place basin in large pan of rapidly boiling water to come two thirds up side of basin. Cover and boil rapidly for 2–2½ hours. Serve straight from the basin, which has been covered with a linen serviette.

Provençal Stuffed Beef

This is a delicious pot roast which can be made in advance and reheated. If prosciutto is unavailable, use coppa.

PREPARATION TIME: *50 minutes*
COOKING TIME: *1–1½ hours*
SERVES 6

❋

1.5 kg fresh silverside, in one piece
200 g prosciutto, chopped
1 cup soft white breadcrumbs
½ cup Italian parsley, chopped
½ cup grated Parmesan cheese
1 egg
2 tablespoons olive oil
3 medium onions, finely chopped
2 sticks celery, finely chopped
2 medium carrots, finely chopped
2 x 400 g cans tomato purée
1 cup red wine
1 tablespoon sugar

1 Slit a deep pocket in silverside. Combine in a bowl prosciutto, breadcrumbs, parsley, Parmesan and egg; press stuffing into pocket and pack firmly. Tie with string to prevent stuffing parting during cooking.
2 Heat oil in a large pan and brown meat on all sides. Remove and place in a casserole.
3 Add onions to skillet and cook until golden in remaining oil, approximately 10 minutes. Add celery and carrots, cover and cook 2 minutes. Add tomato purée, wine and sugar. Simmer sauce 20 minutes. Remove from heat.
4 Pour sauce over silverside, cover and cook in oven at 160° for 1–1½ hours or until meat is cooked and tender. Serve sliced, masked with sauce in which it was cooked. Serve with rice and a green vegetable in season.

Farmhouse Glazed Ham

A quick yet delicious glaze for a whole smoked leg of ham is to combine equal quantities of brown sugar and heated marmalade, add a good pinch of dry mustard and mixed spice and mix well. Stud the fat of the skinned ham with whole cloves and spread brown sugar mixture evenly over ham. Place on a rack in a baking tray, add 1 cup of water to baking tray and bake ham in a moderate oven (180°C) for about 30 minutes. Baste occasionally with pan juices. The glaze will become golden brown and will moisten and flavour the ham beautifully.

Veal Braised with Herbs

Veal Braised with Herbs

Basil, a native of India and South-East Asia, has a sweet, spicy flavour and complements the veal in this recipe.

PREPARATION TIME: 20 minutes
COOKING TIME: 1 hour
SERVES 6

1.5 kg boned leg veal
¼ cup flour
60 g butter
2 medium onions, sliced
200 g prosciutto, cut into strips
2 large tomatoes, peeled, seeded and chopped
1 bunch fresh basil
1½ cups dry white wine
½ cup cream

1 Wash basil, reserve a few leaves for garnish and finely chop remainder. Cut meat into 2 cm cubes and toss in flour. Heat butter in a frying pan. Fry meat cubes a few at a time until brown. Remove.
2 Add onions to remaining butter in pan and fry until golden. Add prosciutto and fry for 2 minutes. Stir through chopped tomatoes, basil and wine. Simmer gently for 5 minutes with the lid on.
3 Add meat to sauce and cook covered for 10 minutes. Remove lid and simmer gently until veal is tender, about 40–45 minutes. Remove meat from sauce and keep warm.
4 Reduce sauce by a third, fold through cream and serve immediately.

Veal can be soaked in milk before use to lighten the flesh if required. As it is a lean cut of meat it is best cooked quickly to prevent drying the flesh, or it can be cooked in a sauce or liquid.

Italian Pot Roast

This is the Italian version of a classic pot roast. Instead of the vegetables being cooked in the pan with the meat, they are prepared with nuts and fruits and placed in a pocket in the meat. Ask the butcher to cut a pocket in the piece of meat.

PREPARATION TIME: 40 minutes
COOKING TIME: 1½ hours
SERVES 4–6

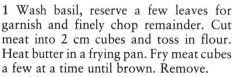

1 x 1.5 kg fillet of veal or beef, pocketed
1 tablespoon olive oil
1 onion, grated
1 clove garlic, crushed
½ small red chilli, chopped finely
1 large carrot, grated
½ cup ground almonds
¼ cup pine nuts
⅓ cup chopped raisins
1 egg yolk
1 tablespoon chutney
extra 1 tablespoon olive oil
2 cups red wine
1 cup beef stock
whole baby potatoes and onions, cooked, for garnish (optional)

1 Remove any fat or sinew from meat.
2 Heat olive oil in pan, add onion, garlic and chilli and fry for 2–3 minutes. Add carrot and cook 2 minutes longer, stirring to combine. Remove from heat; add ground almonds, pine nuts and chopped raisins. Cool slightly and add combined egg yolk and chutney. Mix well to combine.
3 Place stuffing mixture in pocket of meat, pushing in firmly with back of spoon. Secure with string.
4 Heat extra oil in large saucepan. Add meat and cook until well browned all over. Add wine and stock, bring to the boil and then reduce heat. Simmer covered until meat is tender, about 1½ hours.
5 Remove meat from pot. Bring liquid to the boil and boil until reduced and thickened. Serve meat in slices with sauce spooned over. Garnish with whole baby potatoes and onions, if desired.

Ligurian Veal Chops

Liguria is a region in Italy where tiny potatoes and baby squash grow in abundance. This recipe uses both. Veal chops are used here, but any suitable cut of veal will do.

PREPARATION TIME: 20 minutes
COOKING TIME: 45 minutes
SERVES 6

2 tablespoons olive oil
2 cloves garlic, crushed
1 large onion, sliced
6 veal chops, trimmed of any fat

3/4 cup dry white wine
3/4 cup chicken stock
8 small new potatoes
4 large tomatoes, peeled, seeded and chopped
1 tablespoon tomato paste
6–8 small green squash
1/4 teaspoon oregano
1/4 teaspoon marjoram
pepper
fresh rosemary
for garnish

1 Heat oil in heavy-based pan, add garlic and onion and cook 1 minute. Add chops and brown on both sides.

2 Add wine and cook 3–4 minutes. Add stock and potatoes. Place lid on pan and simmer gently 30–35 minutes until meat and potatoes are just cooked.

3 Add tomatoes, tomato paste, squash, oregano and marjoram. Season with salt and pepper. Cook gently with lid off until squash are tender. Garnish with rosemary sprigs. Serve hot with crusty bread.

Ligurian Veal Chops and Italian Pot Roast

Chopped parsley will sprinkle or spread easily without sticking to itself if it is placed in the corner of a clean tea-towel. Twist towel to enclose parsley and remove excess moisture, and then use as required.

Use a potato peeler to obtain long strips of lemon zest, which is the coloured part of the lemon containing all the oils of the lemon and therefore the strongest flavour.

Succotash

Succotash is an American corn and bean dish often served at Thanksgiving dinners. This recipe is a complete meal in itself. It is convenient for entertaining as it can be prepared ahead of time and reheated when it is needed.

PREPARATION TIME: *40 minutes + 2 hours standing*
COOKING TIME: *2 hours*
SERVES 6

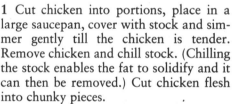

1 x 1.2 kg chicken
4 cups chicken stock
1 kg corned brisket
40 g butter
2 onions, sliced
200 g ham pieces, diced
2 medium potatoes, diced
1 turnip, diced
1 carrot, diced
1 x 400 g can small haricot beans, drained
1 x 400 g can whole kernel corn, drained
1 cup creamed corn
½ cup chopped parsley

1 Cut chicken into portions, place in a large saucepan, cover with stock and simmer gently till the chicken is tender. Remove chicken and chill stock. (Chilling the stock enables the fat to solidify and it can then be removed.) Cut chicken flesh into chunky pieces.
2 Cover corned brisket with cold water, bring gently to the boil and simmer 1–1½ hours or until meat is tender. Remove meat and discard cooking liquid. Cut meat into chunky pieces.
3 Melt butter in a large saucepan and cook onions until transparent. Add ham, potatoes, turnip and carrot. Cover and cook 10 minutes.
4 Add 4 cups of skimmed stock and cook until potatoes are tender.
5 Add chicken meat, brisket, corn and beans. Continue cooking until all ingredients have heated through.
6 Serve in deep bowls, sprinkled with chopped parsley.

Spiced Liver and Kidney

Liver and kidney are excellent sources of protein and iron. They can be prepared in a variety of ways and can be a special breakfast, luncheon or main meal. Offal is best prepared on the day it is purchased.

PREPARATION TIME: *20 minutes + 20 minutes soaking*
COOKING TIME: *45 minutes*
SERVES 4–6

500 g calf's or lamb's liver
2 lamb's kidneys
2 tablespoons olive oil
1 large onion, chopped
1 clove garlic, crushed
1 teaspoon turmeric
1 teaspoon ground coriander
1 teaspoon ground cardamom
½ teaspoon ground cumin
1 x 440 g can peeled tomatoes, chopped, liquid reserved
1 tablespoon lemon juice
1 teaspoon sugar
freshly ground black pepper
2 tablespoons chopped fresh coriander
fine strips lemon rind for garnish

1 Soak liver in salted water for 20 minutes. Drain, dry and remove fine membrane. Slice into paper-thin slices. Skin kidneys, cut in half and remove core. Rinse under cold water; pat dry.
2 Heat oil in pan, add onion and garlic and fry gently until onion is soft. Add turmeric, coriander, cardamom and cumin, cook 2 minutes longer and then add prepared liver and kidney. Fry gently until they change colour.
3 Reduce heat, add chopped tomatoes and reserved liquid from can, lemon juice, sugar and pepper. Cover and simmer for 45 minutes or until meats are tender.
4 Stir in chopped coriander and top with lemon strips just before serving.

Succotash and Spiced Liver and Kidney

OLIVE OIL

The story of olive oil goes back almost 8000 years to when the first trees were cultivated in the Syrian-Iranian region of the Middle East. The oil from the fruit of the olive tree was used as food, fuel and medicine and also for religious ceremonies. Today most of the world's finest olive oil comes from the Mediterranean regions of Italy, France and Spain. To say which particular oil is best is a matter of taste. As with fine wines, the flavour, colour and aroma of olive oils varies according to the type of olive grown, the climate and soil conditions. In fact the wide variety of natural flavours available is what makes olive oil unique among all edible oils.

Pressing Most olive oils are produced from a single 'cold' pressing. The harvested olives are cleaned and ground to a heavy paste using large granite or stainless steel wheels. This opens up the fruit 'cells' that hold the oil. The paste is spread over straw mats which are stacked with a steel plate inserted every five or six mats. The stack is then pressed at room temperature to extract the liquid. This liquid consists of the oil and water from the olives. It is filtered and the oil and water are separated. No chemical process or heating occurs to produce olive oil.

Flavour of Olive Oil The flavour of oil can be categorised as: mild (delicate, light or 'buttery'), semi-fruity (stronger with more taste of the olive), fruity (full-blown olive flavour).

Colour of Olive Oil Olive oil varies in colour from light golden or green to deeper hues of green and gold. Generally the darker, more intensely coloured olive oils have a stronger, more fruity flavour. Like wines, some olive oils are blended from different varieties, and changes in the growing conditions can affect colour and flavour.

Gradings of Olive Oil There are three major grades of olive oil:

Extra Virgin Olive Oil is a virgin olive oil of perfect flavour, colour and aroma. It is produced in small quantities and is the most expensive of all olive oils.

Virgin Olive Oil has less stringent standards for flavour, colour and aroma.

Olive Oil or 100% pure olive oil is a blend of refined olive oil and virgin olive oil. The refined olive oil is made by removing impurities from oils which do not quite meet the standards of the virgin or the extra virgin olive oil. To restore the distinctive flavour, colour and aroma, virgin olive oil is added.

How to Use Olive Oil Try a number of olive oils and decide which one you like best for different uses. To savour the full or delicate flavour of any olive oil, add a little at the final stages of cooking. Olive oil is very stable at high temperatures so it can be used to sauté, stir-fry and deep-fry. It can be reused if filtered after frying but the high heat will result in a loss of flavour.

Always be guided by your own taste buds but, as a general rule, enhance soup, seafood and poultry with mild fruity olive oil. Heartier, more robust dishes, vegetables, pasta and salad greens may taste best with full-flavoured olive oils.

The classic French Vinaigrette and Provençal Aïoli are two of the most popular dressings which use olive oil.

Vinaigrette Dressing

PREPARATION TIME: *15 minutes*
COOKING TIME: *nil*
MAKES *1 cup*

⅓ cup vinegar
1 clove garlic, crushed
2 teaspoons Dijon mustard
salt and freshly ground black pepper
1 cup olive oil

1 Whisk vinegar, garlic, mustard, salt and pepper together in a small bowl until well blended.
2 Gradually whisk oil into vinegar mixture until Vinaigrette is well blended and smooth. Use immediately.

1 Whisk vinegar, garlic, mustard and seasonings well.

2 Gradually whisk in oil until mixture is well blended.

Aïoli

PREPARATION TIME: *20 minutes*
COOKING TIME: *nil*
MAKES *1 cup*

3 cloves garlic, crushed
2 egg yolks
1 cup olive oil
2 teaspoons lemon juice

1 Place garlic and egg yolks in a small clean glass bowl and whisk together until thick and creamy.
2 Gradually add oil, drop by drop, whisking well after each addition. After you have added about a quarter cup oil you may add oil a little more quickly while whisking constantly. After all the oil has been added whisk in the lemon juice. Aïoli can be stored covered in the refrigerator for up to 4 days.

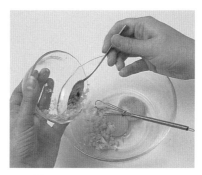

1 Add crushed garlic cloves to egg yolks and whisk until creamy.

2 Add oil drop by drop, whisking well after each addition.

Spiced Olive Oil

PREPARATION TIME: *10 minutes*
COOKING TIME: *nil*
MAKES *2 cups*

1 tablespoon sweet paprika
1 teaspoon ground cumin
1 teaspoon ground fennel
1 teaspoon chilli powder
2 cloves garlic, crushed
500 mL olive oil

Mix paprika, cumin, fennel, chilli powder and garlic with quarter cup olive oil, pour into storage bottle, top with remaining oil and shake well. Store in a cool dark place for 2 weeks before using, to develop flavours.

1 Combine spices and ¼ cup oil; mix well.

2 Pour spice mixture into storage bottle and add remaining oil.

Vegetables & Salads

E VERYWHERE IN THE world, country cooks have devised tempting ways to consume plentiful harvests of vegetables. The English created Pease Porridge, the Syrians liked cabbage rolls. Try Mushrooms Provençal from France, Spanish Pepper Salad, or Layered Bread and Tomato Salad from Italy. They're only a few of the cookery adventures in vegetable meals, side dishes or salads waiting to tempt your appetite here.

Fennel Baked Potatoes, Scottish Parsnip Casserole and Layered Bread and Tomato Salad (page 64)

Scottish Parsnip Casserole

Scottish Parsnip Casserole is an ideal supper dish. Serve it accompanied with damper or crusty bread.

PREPARATION TIME: *20 minutes*
COOKING TIME: *50 minutes*
SERVES 6

1 kg parsnips
1 leek
60 g butter
2 tablespoons brown sugar
freshly ground black pepper
½ teaspoon thyme leaves
1 bunch chives, chopped
6 medium tomatoes, peeled, seeded and chopped
200 g Gruyère cheese, grated
¼ cup cream

1 Preheat oven to 180°C. Grease a large shallow ovenproof dish.
2 Peel and thinly slice parsnips. Wash and thinly slice white part only of the leek.
3 Heat butter in a large pan, add parsnips and leek and cook gently 5 minutes. Stir through brown sugar, freshly ground black pepper and thyme. Remove from heat.
4 Place half the parsnips on the base of an ovenproof dish. Toss tomatoes with chives and arrange half mixture over parsnips. Sprinkle with half the cheese. Layer with remaining ingredients, finishing with cheese. Drizzle over the cream.
5 Bake about 40–50 minutes or until parsnips are tender and cheese forms a crust.

When buying parsnips look for small to medium sized roots which are free of straggly rootlets. Store them in the vegetable section of the refrigerator for up to two weeks. They can be braised, roasted or puréed and enhanced with paprika, ginger, mace or nutmeg. They go well with pork, lamb or veal and combine with other vegetables like carrots, potatoes and sweet potatoes.

Fennel Baked Potatoes

Fennel has a slightly aniseed flavour. The bulb, stalks and feathery leaves are all suitable for flavouring.

PREPARATION TIME: *15 minutes*
COOKING TIME: *60 minutes*
SERVES 6

2 large onions
2 medium fennel bulbs
1 kg large old potatoes

30 g butter
¼ cup olive oil
black pepper

1 Peel onions and cut into thick slices. Remove fennel tops (reserve some for garnish) and any discoloured parts. Cut into 1 cm slices. Peel potatoes and slice into 1 cm slices. Wash fennel and potatoes thoroughly.
2 Preheat oven to 200°C. Add butter and olive oil to large baking pan and heat in oven until hot. Remove from oven, add onion and fennel slices, toss well and cook 20 minutes, turning vegetables over after 10 minutes.
3 Add sliced potatoes and pepper and toss well through fennel mixture, coating the potatoes with the oil in the pan. Bake about 45 minutes or until potatoes are golden brown. Toss occasionally.
4 Allow to stand in a warm place 5–10 minutes before serving. Garnish with fennel leaves.

Layered Bread and Tomato Salad

Balsamic vinegar is a fine Italian vinegar made from a blend of grapes and matured for two years in oak casks before bottling. This gives it its unique flavour and aroma. Red wine vinegar may be substituted.

PREPARATION TIME: *25 minutes*
COOKING TIME: *nil*
SERVES 4–6

6 thick slices crunchy white bread
4 large ripe firm tomatoes, sliced
1 cucumber, peeled and thinly sliced
1 large white onion, sliced
½ cup roughly chopped basil
4 tablespoons olive oil
2 tablespoons balsamic vinegar
coarsely ground pepper

1 Soak bread in cold water for 2–3 minutes. Squeeze bread dry in hands.
2 Arrange layers of bread, tomato, cucumber, onion and basil in bowl.
3 Combine olive oil and vinegar by shaking in a screw-top jar. Pour over salad. Sprinkle top with pepper.
4 Chill well before serving.

Potato, Chick Pea and Tomato Salad

For this salad, potatoes and chick peas are cooked in tomato-flavoured liquid until tender and topped with sultanas for a touch of sweetness to counteract the acid of the tomatoes. The mixture must be well chilled before serving.

PREPARATION TIME: *35 minutes*
COOKING TIME: *nil*
SERVES 6

¼ *cup oil*
3 onions, sliced thickly
½ *cup cooked chick peas*
2 cloves garlic, crushed
6 large potatoes, peeled and sliced
4 large tomatoes, skinned and chopped
3 tablespoons tomato paste
½ *cup tomato purée*
½ *cup water*
freshly ground black pepper
½ *cup sultanas*
½ *cup chopped coriander*

1 Heat oil in pan, add onions and fry until golden brown. Add chick peas and garlic and stir to combine.
2 Add potato slices and cook until they start to colour. Add tomatoes, tomato paste, purée and water; season with black pepper. Bring to the boil and cook gently until potatoes are tender.
3 Add sultanas and coriander; cook 2 minutes longer.
4 Place mixture in serving bowl and cover. Chill well before serving.

Sweet Bean Salad

Beans of all varieties are a staple food the world over, and they are very popular in the middle European countries. There is no need for long soaking or cooking if you use frozen or canned beans. Frozen broad beans have been chosen for this recipe, but any other frozen or canned beans could be used instead.

PREPARATION TIME: *35 minutes*
COOKING TIME: *nil*
SERVES 4

500 g frozen broad beans
2 cloves garlic, crushed
1 leek, sliced
1 large carrot, sliced
½ *cup olive oil*
⅓ *cup cider vinegar*
¼ *cup brown sugar*
¼ *cup chopped parsley*

1 Cook broad beans in boiling water until tender. Drain.
2 Return beans to saucepan, add garlic, leek, carrot and olive oil and cook gently for 5 minutes. Add vinegar and brown sugar and cook 5 minutes longer, making sure brown sugar is dissolved.
3 Chill well before serving. Garnish with chopped parsley.

French Luncheon Salad

As the name implies, this is an attractive array of vegetables suitable as a luncheon meal. It is important not to overcook beans; they should be crisp and a bright green colour. The yoghurt dressing can be prepared the day before.

PREPARATION TIME: *40 minutes*
COOKING TIME: *nil*
SERVES 4

500 g whole baby green beans
1½ cups frozen broad beans, cooked and cooled
2 large tomatoes cut into wedges
1 cup black olives
1 cup croûtons
1 cup low-fat yoghurt
½ *cup mayonnaise*
1 teaspoon French mustard
1 tablespoon chopped dill

1 Cook green beans in boiling water 2–3 minutes, remove and plunge into ice-cold water. Drain and pat dry with paper towel.
2 Arrange green beans, broad beans, tomatoes, olives and croûtons in decorative pattern on a large flat platter.
3 Combine yoghurt, mayonnaise, mustard and dill. Mix well. Pour over green beans on platter. Chill well before serving.
Note: Beans can be cooked, covered, in microwave for 1½ minutes on High. Allow to cool completely before using.

If you don't own a garlic crusher, do not despair: garlic can be crushed using a large sharp knife. Simply place garlic clove on board, place the flat part of the knife on top and press down firmly. Remove papery skin. Sprinkle garlic with a little salt and, using flat edge of knife blade, work salt and garlic to a paste.

Garlic can impart its unique flavour and aroma in many ways in cooking. For full-bodied flavour crush garlic with a garlic crusher to release the essential oils, while to give a subtle flavour add a whole uncut garlic clove to your dishes while cooking. To flavour a dish slightly, peel a clove of garlic and slice thinly, add the slices to oil and cook gently until garlic just begins to colour. Then add remaining ingredients.

Spanish Pepper Salad

This recipe uses sweet peppers or capsicums. The capsicums are skinned, which results in softer texture and more delicate flavour. The capsicums may be prepared the day before serving and covered with dressing. Add orange on the day of serving.

PREPARATION TIME: *40 minutes*
COOKING TIME: *nil*
SERVES 4

2 large red capsicums, halved
2 large green capsicums, halved
½ cup chopped chives
⅓ cup olive oil
⅓ cup white wine vinegar
2 large oranges, skin removed, thickly
sliced
½ cup large green olives
¼ cup large black olives

1 Place capsicums under hot grill and cook until skin becomes black. Remove capsicums and put into a plastic bag. Leave until cool enough to handle. Remove from bag and rub away all skin — you may need to rinse under cold water. Cut capsicums into thick slices.
2 Combine chives, olive oil and white wine vinegar. Arrange capsicums, oranges and olives in serving bowl. Pour over dressing. Chill well before serving.
Note: To remove all skin from orange, including the white part or pith, hold orange firmly on a cutting board and, using large sharp knife, cut from top to base until all skin is removed and only flesh remains. If pith is left it will impart a bitter flavour.

Olive oil was central to the early economic development of the Mediterranean civilisations. Ancient Greece produced more olive oil than its people could use and from at least 6000 BC it also produced earthenware jars which were used to store and transport olive oil. By trading olive oil for wheat, Greece set up a cycle of economic growth which greatly contributed to the flowering of Greek civilisation.

Potato, Chick Pea and Tomato Salad and Sweet Bean Salad (page 65)

Vine Leaves Stuffed with Rice

Vine leaves are used mainly in Middle Eastern countries to encase food. Delicatessens sell vine leaves in cans and packets. They have been processed and only require rinsing before use.

PREPARATION TIME: *40 minutes*
COOKING TIME: *20–30 minutes*
MAKES 16 *parcels*

1 cup cooked brown rice
2 tablespoons toasted pine nuts
¼ cup chopped mint
125 g fresh dates, diced
1 tablespoon olive oil
250 g lean lamb, minced
1 clove garlic, crushed
1 tablespoon lemon juice
pepper
freshly grated nutmeg
16 vine leaves, rinsed and dried
2 tablespoons water or wine
1 tablespoon olive oil
LEMON HONEY SAUCE
25 g butter
1 tablespoon honey
1 tablespoon flour
200 mL chicken stock
rind and juice of 1 large lemon
freshly ground pepper
grated nutmeg

1 Combine rice, pine nuts, mint and dates in a mixing bowl.
2 Heat olive oil in a pan until hot, add lamb and cook quickly. Add garlic and fry 1 minute. Pour over lemon juice and add pepper and freshly ground nutmeg.
3 Stir meat mixture through rice and allow to cool. Spoon stuffing onto vine leaves and roll into small parcels. Place parcels in a shallow, well greased casserole in one layer. Combine water and oil, shaking well; pour over prepared vine leaves.
4 Cover casserole dish with lid or foil. Bake about 20 minutes at 180°C.
5 To make Lemon Honey Sauce, melt butter in a saucepan, add honey and brown slightly. Stir through flour. Remove from heat and stir until smooth. Slowly blend in stock, lemon juice and rind, return to heat and stir continuously until sauce boils and thickens. Adjust seasonings and pour over vine leaves just before serving.

Eggplant with Pesto of Green Olives and Capers (page 68)
French Luncheon Salad (page 65), Spanish Pepper Salad and Vine Leaves Stuffed with Rice

67

Eggplant with Pesto of Green Olives and Capers

This tasty recipe needs to be prepared several hours before it is required. It is a chilled eggplant slice, suitable for entrée, supper or a luncheon dish.

PREPARATION TIME: *30 minutes + 7 hours standing and chilling*
COOKING TIME: *20 minutes*
SERVES 6

1 kg medium-sized eggplant
salt
olive oil
3 hard-boiled eggs
¾ cup chopped green olives
1 tablespoon chopped basil leaves
2 tablespoons capers
6 shallots
50 g hard pecorino cheese
¼ cup olive oil
50 mL red wine vinegar
toasted sesame seeds and basil leaves to garnish

1 Peel eggplant and cut into 5 mm slices lengthwise. Sprinkle with salt and allow to stand 60 minutes in a plastic colander so that all liquid can drain away from the eggplant. Rinse. Remove and dry thoroughly with kitchen paper.
2 Heat olive oil in frying pan and fry eggplant until golden brown on both sides. Remove and drain well and allow to cool.
3 In a food processor combine all the remaining ingredients except the garnish; the mixture should be creamy. Place a layer of eggplant in a well oiled 20 x 30 cm shallow dish. Spread with half the egg mixture. Top with overlapping slices of eggplant, spread with remaining egg mixture and finish with a layer of sliced eggplant. Sprinkle with sesame seeds and chill well at least 6 hours.
4 Slice and serve garnished with basil.

The eggplant or aubergine is believed to have been introduced to the Mediterranean area by the Arabs during the Dark Ages. It was not well known in Europe until the sixteenth century. As they are high in water content eggplants are best salted before use. This also removes the bitter after-taste.

1 Sprinkle sliced eggplant with salt and stand in a colander for 60 minutes to drain away any bitter juices.

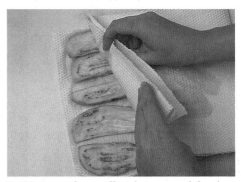

2 Rinse eggplant well with water and dry thoroughly with absorbent kitchen paper.

3 Cook eggplant in olive oil on both sides until golden brown; drain on absorbent paper.

4 Place a single layer of eggplant evenly over the base of a shallow dish and top with egg mixture.

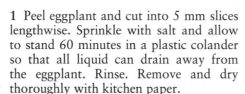

Stuffed Zucchini Provençal

Basil or dill can be used in this French recipe. The French make good use of such herbs for their characteristic flavours.

PREPARATION TIME: *30 minutes*
COOKING TIME: *40 minutes*
SERVES 4

8 medium zucchini
½ cup mushrooms
30 g butter
2 tablespoons lemon juice
pepper
½ cup cooked rice
2 tablespoons chopped chives
2 tablespoons chopped basil or dill
½ cup grated Gruyère cheese

¼ cup grated Gruyère cheese, extra
lemon slices to garnish

1 Preheat oven to 180°C. Scrape zucchini skins lightly, cut off ends and cut through lengthwise into half. Score the flesh and parboil 3–5 minutes. Drain, cool and scoop out flesh, leaving enough on the skins to support filling. Reserve zucchini pulp.
2 Slice mushrooms and fry in melted butter; cook until all liquids have evaporated. Add lemon juice and 1 cup chopped zucchini pulp; cook 2 minutes. Season with freshly ground black pepper.
3 Combine cooked rice in a bowl with chives, basil and Gruyère cheese. Add cooked mushrooms to rice filling and combine well. Pile into zucchini cases and sprinkle with extra cheese. Arrange in greased shallow ovenproof dish.
4 Bake in preheated oven for 30 minutes or until filling heats through and cheese melts. Serve garnished with basil or dill and lemon slices.

Stuffed Zucchini Provençal

Modern technology now enables us to have fresh herbs almost all year round. When purchased, fresh herbs need to be washed to remove any soil and then shaken to remove most of the water. Store in a plastic bag for up to one week in the refrigerator.

Clockwise from top left: Hearty Vegetable Casserole, Mushrooms Provençal and Irish Potato Pikelets (page 72)

Hearty Vegetable Casserole

Celeriac is a variety of celery cultivated for its thick, turnip-like root. If unavailable, use stalk celery. Any seasonal vegetable can be added to this casserole.

PREPARATION TIME: *35 minutes*
COOKING TIME: *40 minutes*
SERVES 6

1 medium celeriac
1 medium fennel bulb
12 baby onions, peeled
12 baby carrots
300 g sweet potato
250 g button mushrooms
½ bunch English spinach
6 yellow button squash
100 g snow peas
60 g butter
2 tablespoons chopped basil
2 tablespoons chopped chives
½ cup white wine
½ cup chicken stock

1 Peel and chop celeriac into 2 cm dice. Trim and remove root from fennel and chop roughly. Bring a saucepan of water to the boil and blanch celeriac, fennel and onions about 5 minutes. Drain. Preheat oven to 180°C.
2 Wash and scrape carrots, peel sweet potato and slice thinly, wipe over mushrooms. Rinse and roughly chop spinach. Rinse squash and remove green top and bottom. Rinse and string snow peas.
3 Heat butter in a pan and cook onions until golden. Remove from pan. Add spinach, cover and simmer 2 minutes. Toss through basil and chives. Remove from pan, place in greased casserole. Reserve liquid.
4 Add wine and chicken stock to the pan with spinach liquid. Bring to the boil. Remove from heat.
5 Arrange vegetables, except snow peas, over spinach in casserole dish. Pour over sauce, cover and bake in a moderately hot oven for about 30 minutes or until vegetables are tender. In last 5 minutes scatter snow peas over the top, cover and continue cooking. Serve immediately.

Mushrooms Provençal

Mushrooms can be used in many ways. This recipe takes the form of a Mushroom Gratin with a crisp topping.

PREPARATION TIME: *45 minutes*
COOKING TIME: *20 minutes*
SERVES 4–6

500 g mushrooms
1 medium leek
60 g butter
1 clove garlic, crushed
juice and grated rind of 1 lemon
pepper
freshly grated nutmeg
½ cup chopped parsley
1½ cups soft wholemeal breadcrumbs
2 tablespoons olive oil
1 whole clove garlic

1 Wipe over mushrooms and cut into slices. Trim leek and wash well; cut into fine shreds. Preheat oven to 200°C, and grease a 20 cm ovenproof dish.
2 Melt butter in a heavy-based pan, add leek, cover and cook, stirring, for 5 minutes over a low heat. Add sliced mushrooms and toss to coat in leek and butter mixture. Cover and cook 10 minutes. Remove lid, add crushed garlic and lemon rind and cook until most of the juices have evaporated, about 15–20 minutes.
3 Pour over lemon juice, reduce and season with pepper, parsley and nutmeg. Fold through ½ cup of the breadcrumbs. Spoon into prepared casserole dish.
4 Heat olive oil in pan; when hot add whole garlic and cook until garlic browns. Remove and discard the garlic. Add remaining breadcrumbs to oil and toss to coat crumbs.
5 Sprinkle crumbs over mushroom mixture. Bake in prepared oven until mixture has heated through and crumb topping is crisp, about 20 minutes.

Celeriac is a member of the celery family. It goes by many names: celery knob, celery root and turnip-rooted celery. It is globular in shape, brown outside with creamy white flesh, and is best peeled just before cooking, as it darkens quickly once peeled. Choose small celeriac as they are more tender than the big ones. It is delicious boiled and served with butter and paprika or used in any vegetable dish. You may also serve it uncooked in salads as you would celery.

Stuffed Baked Onions (page 73) and Crispy Pita Bread Salad

Irish Potato Pikelets

Pikelets from Ireland — of course they contain potato, Ireland's staple food. This is a basic mixture that can be served either savoury or sweet. Make sure that the potatoes are very well mashed, creamy and free from lumps.

PREPARATION TIME: *25 minutes*
COOKING TIME: *20 minutes*
MAKES *20–24 pikelets*

1 cup grated raw potato
1 cup cooked mashed potato
½ cup self-raising flour
½ teaspoon bicarbonate of soda
¼ teaspoon nutmeg
2 tablespoons melted butter
1 teaspoon vinegar
¾ cup milk

1 Squeeze raw grated potato to remove excess liquid and combine with mashed potato, sifted flour, bicarbonate of soda and nutmeg.

2 Stir vinegar into milk and allow to stand 2 minutes. Add melted butter and milk to potato mixture. Stir gently until well combined.
3 Drop spoonfuls of mixture onto well greased pan. Cook on both sides until golden brown and cooked through.
4 Serve hot as accompaniment to any baked meat or vegetable dish.

Crispy Pita Bread Salad

This is a Syrian peasant salad that can accompany other dishes or stand alone as a luncheon or supper dish.

PREPARATION TIME: *35 minutes*
COOKING TIME: *10 minutes*
SERVES 6

3 small pita breads
½ cup chopped mint

In Greece, Italy and Middle Eastern countries flat leavened and unleavened bread is still prepared and kneaded at home and then sent to the local village bakery to be baked. Women brand their bread with their own mark and send their children with it to the bakery where the children wait and watch patiently as the bread is baked amongst the many other village loaves.

2/3 cup chopped parsley
1 cup chopped spring onions
1/3 cup olive oil
1/4 cup lemon juice
freshly ground pepper
2 small red onions
2 sticks celery
2 cucumbers
3 tomatoes
1 red capsicum
1 teaspoon sugar

1 Split pita bread and place on a tray. Bake pita in preheated oven at 200°C for 10 minutes or until crisp and brown.
2 Combine mint, parsley, spring onions, oil, lemon juice and pepper. Allow to stand while preparing salad ingredients.
3 Peel and thinly slice the red onions; chop the celery; peel, seed and slice the cucumbers. Cut tomatoes in halves, squeeze gently to remove seeds and chop the flesh. Cut capsicum into thin strips. Break pita bread into small pieces.
4 Combine all salad ingredients and toss well. Add the split pita bread about 10 minutes before serving.

Stuffed Baked Onions

The baked onions can be prepared well in advance and cooked just before serving. Stuffed vegetables are suitable for entrées or main course dishes.

PREPARATION TIME: *50 minutes*
COOKING TIME: *30 minutes*
SERVES 4

4 large brown onions
200 g pancetta
6 anchovy fillets, mashed
1 tablespoon capers
2 tablespoons Italian parsley
1 tablespoon olive oil
2 tablespoons pine nuts, toasted
1 clove garlic, crushed
1 cup soft white breadcrumbs
2 tablespoons olive oil, extra

1 Peel onions, cover with cold water and simmer 30 minutes or until onions are tender. Drain; cut in half horizontally. Remove the centre pieces to give a hollow in which to place filling. Finely chop the removed pieces of onion.

2 Finely shred the pancetta and combine with chopped onion, anchovies, capers, finely chopped parsley, 1 tablespoon olive oil and pine nuts. Press firmly into onion halves and place in an ovenproof dish which has been lightly oiled.
3 Heat extra olive oil in a saucepan and add garlic. Fry quickly and toss through breadcrumbs until all crumbs are well coated with garlic oil. Sprinkle over stuffed onion halves. Bake at 200°C for 30 minutes until golden brown and cooked through. Serve garnished with parsley.

Hot Chick Pea Salad

Chick peas are also known as Spanish beans or garbanzos. They require long soaking and cooking to become tender, but they are certainly worth the effort. Try them in this French-inspired hot salad.

PREPARATION TIME: *1 hour + 1 hour standing*
COOKING TIME: *nil*
SERVES 4

1 cup dried chick peas
2 bay leaves
1 onion cut in quarters
1/3 cup olive oil
3 cloves garlic, crushed
1 large red onion, chopped
1/3 cup chopped parsley
1/2 cup orange juice
2 tablespoons red wine vinegar
2 teaspoons grated orange rind
1/3 cup chopped parsley, extra, for garnish

1 Place chick peas in large saucepan, cover with cold water and bring to the boil. Remove from heat, cover and allow to stand for 1 hour. Drain, cover with fresh water, add bay leaves and onion, cover and cook for 45 minutes or until chick peas are tender. Drain.
2 Heat oil in pan, add garlic and cook gently 2–3 minutes. Add drained peas; cook 2–3 minutes. Add onion, parsley, orange juice, red wine vinegar and orange rind. Cook 2–3 minutes.
3 Serve hot or at room temperature, garnished with extra chopped parsley.
Note: To save on cooking time, 2 x 375 g cans of chick peas can be used. Drain well before using.

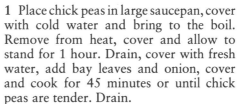

Hot Chick Pea Salad

For easy and successful grating of orange zest, choose finest part of grater and cover with piece of greaseproof paper. Grate skin of orange just to coloured part — zest will be collected on paper. Remove. Use table knife or brush to collect before adding to recipe.

Marsala Celery Braise

Rigani is a Greek herb which complements this dish. If it is unavailable, substitute marjoram or oregano.

PREPARATION TIME: *30 minutes*
COOKING TIME: *35 minutes*
SERVES 6

1 bunch celery
4 whole cloves
2 bay leaves
30 g butter
2 rashers bacon, rind removed and cut into strips
2 onions, diced
2 carrots, diced
2 cups chicken stock
1 teaspoon rigani leaves
2 tablespoons Marsala
2 tablespoons cream
1 tablespoon cornflour

Marsala is an Italian fortified wine originally manufactured in the town of Marsala in Sicily. It is used in both sweet and savoury dishes.

1 Cut celery into 5 cm lengths. Bring a large saucepan of water to the boil, add cloves and bay leaves and boil 1 minute. Add celery and cook 5 minutes. Drain and remove cloves and bay leaves.
2 In a large pan melt the butter, add bacon strips and cook until crisp. Add carrots and onions and cook until onions have softened.
3 Add chicken stock, rigani and celery, reduce heat and simmer 30 minutes or until celery is tender. Lift celery out with a slotted spoon and arrange on a serving dish. Keep warm.
4 Blend cornflour with Marsala and cream, add to stock mixture, stir, bring to boil and simmer 3 minutes. Pour over celery to serve.

Pease Porridge

Pease porridge hot, pease porridge cold; some like it in the pot — but not quite nine days old! This variation on the very old rhyme still does not do justice to this substantial but delicately flavoured vegetable dish. Originally it was used as a meat replacement but it can also be served as a vegetable accompaniment.

PREPARATION TIME: *1½ hours + 2 hours soaking*

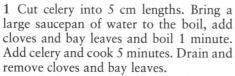

COOKING TIME: *20 minutes*
SERVES 4–6

500 g green split peas
1 L water
1 leek, cut into thin rounds
1 bouquet garni
⅓ cup cream
2 egg yolks
¼ teaspoon nutmeg
¼ teaspoon black pepper
1 cup fresh white breadcrumbs
1 tablespoon butter

1 Rinse peas thoroughly, cover with cold water and leave to soak about 2 hours. Drain.
2 Place peas in saucepan with 1 L water, leek and bouquet garni. Bring to the boil and boil until peas are soft, about 1 hour.
3 Drain peas and remove bouquet garni. Mash or blend pea mixture, cool slightly and beat in cream, egg yolks, nutmeg and pepper.
4 Put into greased deep casserole, top with breadcrumbs, dot with butter and bake at 180°C until breadcrumbs are golden brown, about 20 minutes.

Cabbage Rolls

This nutritious dish is relatively inexpensive to make. The yoghurt sauce is a refreshing accompaniment to the cumin-flavoured filling.

PREPARATION TIME: *40 minutes*
COOKING TIME: *1½ hours*
SERVES 6

12 large cabbage leaves
500 g potatoes
60 g ghee
2 medium onions, thinly sliced
1 tablespoon ground cumin
1 tablespoon ground coriander
1 teaspoon ground ginger
1 white turnip, diced
½ cup diced celery
1 cup chicken stock
1 x 400 g can cannellini beans
1 x 400 g can chick peas
pepper
30 g butter, melted

SAUCE
1½ cups plain yoghurt
½ cup chopped mint
1 tablespoon cornflour
½ cup chicken stock
1 tablespoon lemon juice

1 Blanch cabbage leaves until just tender. Remove centre core from each cabbage leaf. Peel and chop potatoes into small pieces.
2 Melt ghee in a large saucepan and cook onion slices until golden. Add cumin, coriander and ginger and cook, stirring, 2 minutes. Add turnip, celery, potatoes and stock. Cover saucepan and cook gently until potatoes are tender. Add beans and chick peas and simmer until liquid has

reduced and mixture is thick. Season with freshly ground pepper.
3 Spoon potato mixture evenly into cabbage leaves and roll each leaf to form a cylinder. Secure with toothpick. Place in casserole dish, brush with melted butter and drizzle over ¼ cup water. Cover with foil and bake at 180°C for 45–50 minutes.
4 To prepare Sauce, combine yoghurt and mint in a saucepan and warm gently. Blend cornflour with stock, add to yoghurt and cook until mixture thickens. Do not boil too long as sauce will curdle. Just before serving add lemon juice.
5 To serve lift the cabbage rolls onto a warm serving plate and pour over the yoghurt sauce. Garnish with lemon slices and chopped parsley, if desired.

Clockwise from top left: Pease Porridge, Marsala Celery Braise and Cabbage Rolls

HERBS

Pungent and aromatic herbs give distinctive flavour to foods, with every country having its favourites. Italian cuisine is famous for its use of basil, oregano and rosemary to dress pasta, pizza and vegetables. The French favour tarragon to enhance the classic Béarnaise and Hollandaise sauces, while in Provençal French cookery zesty herbs like thyme, marjoram, sage, rosemary and fennel add flavour to hearty country dishes. The traditional bouquet garni is a famous French herb bouquet: bay leaves are an essential ingredient, the accompanying herbs being parsley, marjoram and thyme. They are usually tied together and put into sauces, stews, casseroles and soup. The regional dishes of the Middle East, Spain and Greece use fennel, garlic, mint and dill to add zest to their dishes.

Preserving Herbs

Store fresh sprigs of herbs in plastic wrap, damp absorbent paper or plastic bags in the refrigerator for up to a week. For longer periods chop fresh herbs finely, place in ice cube tray, cover with water and freeze. When needed, remove ice cubes and stir into hot cooking — they will melt in a few minutes. Use a little less of frozen herbs than of fresh as freezing them tends to give them a bitter flavour.

Aromatic herb oils are another way of using fresh herbs when they are in season. The flavoured oil can be used to baste meats and seafood while they are cooking or it may be used as a base oil in a vinaigrette dressing or to dress hot vegetables.

Herbed salt is a zesty condiment to serve with seafood, barbecued meats and salads. Use a good quality dried herb or a mix of herbs — try rosemary, oregano, sage, thyme or rigani. Store the herb salt in an airtight container in a cool dark place.

How to Dry Herbs

To dry fresh herbs when supplies are abundant, try one of these methods. The faster the drying process, the more flavourful the dried results will be.

Conventional Oven Method

Place clean dry herb sprigs on foil-lined tray. Cook at the oven's lowest setting until herbs are dry and brittle to touch — this may take up to 12 hours. Strip leaves from stems, place in clean, dry jars and seal with airtight lids.

Microwave Oven Method
Strip fresh leaves from stems and scatter on absorbent paper. Place in microwave and cook on High in 650 watt oven for about 3 minutes. Drying time will vary between different herbs.

Air Drying Method
Tie small bunches of herbs with string and hang in a warm, dry airy place until dry. This will take up to two weeks. Do not attempt this method when the weather is humid.

Herbed Oils

PREPARATION TIME: *10 minutes*
+ 5 days standing
COOKING TIME: *2 minutes*
MAKES *2 cups*

2 cups vegetable oil
10–12 tablespoons chopped
fresh herbs
sprigs of fresh herbs

1 Heat oil in a double saucepan (to prevent oil breaking down). Add herbs. Remove from heat, cool, cover and store in a cool dark place for 5 days.
2 Strain into a sterilised bottle. Add a fresh sprig of herb. Seal and store in a cool place.
Note: Use basil, sage, rosemary, lemon thyme and garlic or experiment with other herbs of your choice.

1 Heat oil in a double saucepan or a bowl over simmering water. Add herbs.

2 Strain herbed oil into a bottle. Add a fresh herb sprig.

Herb Butter

PREPARATION TIME: *30 minutes*
COOKING TIME: *nil*
MAKES *15 slices*

125 g butter, at room
temperature
3 tablespoons chopped fresh
herb (e.g., tarragon, chives, basil,
parsley, dill, oregano) or
2 teaspoons dried herb
1 tablespoon finely chopped
onion
1 tablespoon lemon juice
freshly ground black pepper

1 Beat all ingredients together in a small bowl.
2 Form mixture into a 15 cm log on a sheet of aluminium foil. Wrap up tightly. Twist ends of foil to compress butter.
3 Place in the freezer to store (for up to 2 months).
4 Cut into 1 cm slices to serve. Place a pat on grilled meat, fish or chicken.

1 Form herbed butter mixture into a 15 cm log on a sheet of aluminium foil.

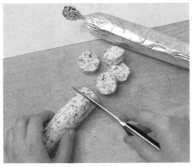

2 Herbed Butter can be frozen for up to 2 months. Cut into slices to serve.

Herbed Salt

PREPARATION TIME: *20 minutes*
COOKING TIME: *nil*
MAKES *500g*

2 teaspoons dried rosemary
2 teaspoons dried oregano
500 g sea salt
2 cloves peeled garlic

1 Using a mortar and pestle or a blender lightly pound rosemary and oregano. Add a little salt and mix to a fine powder.
2 Combine herbs with remaining salt, pour into a jar, push the garlic cloves into centre of salt and cover. Store in a cool dark place for one week before using.

1 Pound dried rosemary, oregano and salt to a fine powder.

2 Pour herbed salt into a storage jar, add garlic cloves and cover.

Breads from Other Lands

Today the scent of warm bread as it comes from the oven and the sight of its golden freshness are as appealing to the senses as ever they were. The basket of recipes we present you with here shows how versatile and delicious those peasant breads can be. Old favourites such as Irish Soda Bread, Molasses Cornbread, English Muffins and Country Milk Rolls and the fascinating flavours and textures of Italian Focaccia, Armenian Flatbreads or Indian Paratha will bring the excitement of country bread from other lands to your kitchen and inspire you to sample them all.

Fruit and Nut Flowerpot Bread, Irish Soda Bread (page 80) and Cornbread Muffins (page 85)

Irish Soda Bread

This is a yeast-free bread: bicarbonate of soda, cream of tartar and buttermilk form the leavening agent. It is a light bread with a scone-like texture. Originally this bread was baked on a griddle.

PREPARATION TIME: *15 minutes*
COOKING TIME: *20 minutes*
MAKES *1 x 25 cm round loaf*

3 cups plain white flour
2 cups plain wholemeal flour
1 teaspoon salt
3 level teaspoons bicarbonate of soda
1½ level tablespoons cream of tartar
1 tablespoon sugar
60 g butter
2¼ cups buttermilk

1 Preheat oven to 220°C and grease a flat tray.
2 Sift flours, salt, bicarbonate of soda, cream of tartar and sugar into a large mixing bowl. Rub through the butter. Pour in the buttermilk and mix with the hands to form a light dough.
3 Turn onto a lightly floured surface and knead lightly. Shape into a ball and place on prepared tray. Flatten into a round 3 cm thick. Cut the round into quarters and push them apart a little so that there is about 15 mm between them.
4 Dust lightly with a little extra wholemeal flour and bake in preheated oven for about 30 minutes.

Buttermilk was originally the whey from unpasteurised milk in the butter-making process. Today, as milk is pasteurised before being churned into butter, it has a special culture added to give the characteristic tang. Buttermilk has the same nutritional value as skimmed milk.

Molasses Cornbread

This bread with its cake-like texture comes from America, where molasses is used extensively in both sweet and savoury baking. Molasses is used in this recipe to give the bread its rich flavour and dark colour.

PREPARATION TIME: *30 minutes + 1 hour standing*
COOKING TIME: *40 minutes*
MAKES *1 large loaf*

2 cups plain flour
1 cup rye flour

1 cup cornmeal
1 x 7 g sachet dried yeast
1½ cups milk, scalded and cooled to lukewarm
¼ cup molasses
80 g butter, melted
milk for glazing

1 Combine flours, cornmeal and yeast in large basin. Make well in centre and stir in combined milk, molasses and melted butter. Beat with wooden spoon until mixture starts to leave side of basin.
2 Place in lightly oiled basin, cover with plastic wrap and leave in warm position until mixture doubles in bulk.
3 Punch dough down. Place on floured board; knead. Press out into rectangle and roll up as for Swiss roll. Put into well greased large loaf tin. Place in warm position until mixture rises to top of tin. Glaze with milk.
4 Bake at 180°C for 30–40 minutes until bread sounds hollow when tapped.

Fruit and Nut Flowerpot Bread

A spicy fruit and nut dough baked in terracotta pots, giving a thick crunchy crust. Pots must be washed thoroughly and dried and then seasoned. Coat them with oil inside and out and bake in hot oven for 5 minutes. Allow to cool; repeat process 3 or 4 times. The pots are then ready to use. Place square of aluminium foil in base and grease with melted butter.

PREPARATION TIME: *35 minutes + 1 hour standing*
COOKING TIME: *30 minutes*
MAKES *4 pots*

30 g fresh yeast or 2 x 7 g sachets dry yeast
¼ cup melted butter
2 tablespoons honey
2 cups warm water
5 cups plain flour
2 teaspoons cinnamon
2 cups chopped pecans
1½ cups sultanas
milk for glazing
4 x 10 cm diameter terracotta pots

1 Combine yeast, melted butter, honey and warm water. Let stand in warm position for 10 minutes.

2 Sift flour and cinnamon into large basin; mix in pecans and sultanas. Make well in centre and add yeast mixture to form a soft dough. Place on floured board and knead for 3 minutes. Return to lightly oiled basin, brush top with oil and cover with plastic wrap. Stand in warm position until double in bulk.

3 Punch down. Divide dough into four even pieces. Knead lightly, shape each into a ball and place in well greased pots. Stand in warm position until dough comes to top of pot. Glaze with milk.

4 Bake at 180°C for 25–30 minutes until the loaves are well browned and sound hollow when tapped.

Note: If terracotta flowerpots are not available, the dough may be baked in two well greased loaf tins.

Molasses Cornbread

Clockwise from back; Lavosh Bread, Black Bread and Crispy Seeded Flatbreads (page 88)

Polenta

Polenta is a cornbread accompaniment served with many Italian dishes. It can either be served like mashed potatoes or cooled completely and later sliced and grilled or fried.

PREPARATION TIME: *10 minutes*
COOKING TIME: *10–15 minutes*
SERVES 6–8

3 cups milk
3 cups water
90 g butter
½ teaspoon salt
½ teaspoon ground nutmeg
2 tablespoons dried onion flakes
1⅔ cups cornmeal
¾ cup semolina

1 In a large saucepan bring the water and milk to the boil. Add butter, seasonings and onion flakes. Simmer two minutes.
2 Sprinkle through cornmeal and semolina and stir continuously until mixture becomes thick and porridge-like and starts to leave the sides of the saucepan, about 15 minutes.
3 Serve as an accompaniment to other foods, or pack into a 23 x 30 cm shallow pan which has been greased with butter or oil. Chill until firm, cut into squares and grill or fry until golden. Serve hot.

Black Bread

This bread is similar to pumpernickel. It is made without yeast and keeps for up to two weeks. Serve buttered and top with cream cheese, smoked salmon and chopped cucumber.

PREPARATION TIME: *15 minutes*
COOKING TIME: *1 hour*
MAKES 2 loaves

1 teaspoon salt
1 kg cornmeal
2 cups rye flour
5 tablespoons molasses
3 tablespoons malt powder
2 tablespoons water
1 teaspoon bicarbonate of soda

3 cups sour milk
1 tablespoon caraway seeds

1 Preheat oven to 160°C. Grease two bread tins with margarine. Combine salt, cornmeal and rye flour in a large bowl.
2 Mix molasses, malt and water together and heat until just warm. (This thins the mixture and makes it easier to mix with the flour.) Combine molasses mixture with bicarbonate of soda, sour milk and caraway seeds, add to the cornmeal and rye flour and mix well.
3 Pour into bread tins and bake slowly for 45–60 minutes. Cool before using.

Lavash Bread

Flatbreads of many varieties are used throughout the Middle East. Lavosh bread is a flaky pastry bread suitable for dips or for spreading with toppings. It makes a delightful snack.

PREPARATION TIME: *20 minutes + 1 hour chilling time*
COOKING TIME: *10 minutes*
MAKES 3 *rectangular breads*

500 g plain flour
50 g unsalted butter
1 teaspoon salt
1 teaspoon sugar
2 eggs
100 mL milk
2 tablespoons poppy seeds
2 tablespoons sesame seeds

1 Sift flour, salt and sugar into a bowl and rub in the butter with the fingertips until mixture resembles breadcrumbs.
2 Lightly beat the eggs with the milk. Add all but 1 tablespoon of this mixture to the dry ingredients. Mix well to form a firm dough. Wrap and refrigerate one hour before rolling out.
3 Preheat oven to 200°C. Grease three scone trays.
4 Cut dough into three pieces. Roll each piece to form a thin rectangle. Place on prepared trays, brush with reserved egg mixture and sprinkle with combined poppy and sesame seeds. Bake in preheated oven for about 10 minutes or until bread is golden. Cool.
5 Break into pieces to serve.

Polenta is one of the staple starches of northern Italy. Although generally made of maize flour, it can be made of chestnut flour, ground barley, buckwheat or semolina. Traditionally it was cooked in a large copper pan called a paiolo.

Breads and pastries often require kneading. This process develops the protein structure in the flour and contributes to the structure and texture of the completed bread or pastry.

Indian Spinach Paratha

This is an Indian bread which is similar to pita or pocket bread but it does not have the yeast leavener.

PREPARATION TIME: *45 minutes + 1¼ hours standing*
COOKING TIME: *40 minutes*
MAKES *20 small (12 cm) rounds*

2 cups plain white flour
¾ cup plain wholemeal flour
1 teaspoon ground cumin
1 teaspoon salt
1 x 250 g packet frozen spinach, thawed
60 g ghee, melted
½ cup warm water
¼ cup vegetable oil
oil for deep frying

1 Sift the flours with cumin and salt into a large bowl. Squeeze the frozen spinach, removing as much water as possible.
2 Make a well in the centre of the flour, add melted ghee, water and spinach. Knead through the mixture until well combined. Mixture should come together to form a soft ball.
3 Lift the dough out of the bowl onto a floured surface and knead for about 15 minutes until mixture becomes smooth, glossy and elastic. Cover with plastic wrap and rest for 60 minutes before shaping.
4 Roll into a log shape 35 cm long × 4 cm thick. Cut into 20 pieces. Work with one piece of dough at a time and keep the remaining pieces covered to prevent them drying.
5 Roll each piece of dough into a 12 cm round and brush lightly with oil. Make a slit from the centre of the circle to the edge. Starting at the cut edge, roll the dough to form a cone shape. Pick it up to form a dome and press in the centre to flatten. Reroll to form 12 cm circle. Place on a lightly floured tray; cover with towel. Continue to shape remaining dough. Allow shaped bread to rest 10 minutes before cooking.
6 Heat oil in a frying pan until hot. Fry spinach bread one at a time. The bread will sink to the bottom and then float to the top as it cooks. Cook until puffed and crisp. Serve immediately.

Indian Spinach Paratha

Spinach has dark green leaves and slender green stalks and, although delicious raw in salads, wilts very quickly and must be used when freshly picked. Sometimes silver beet is used as a substitute.

1 *Roll dough into log shape, cut into 20 evenly sized pieces and roll each piece into a ball.*

2 *Roll out each ball into a 12 cm round and brush each with oil.*

3 *Make a slit with a small sharp knife from the centre of the circle to the edge. Roll the edge to make a cone shape.*

4 *Press each cone shape down from the centre to flatten. Reroll each to form a 12 cm circle. Allow bread to rest 10 minutes before cooking.*

Cornbread Muffins

Try these as a breakfast treat. Serve them as they are or use them to accompany bacon and eggs or sausages and tomatoes for a hearty country breakfast.

PREPARATION TIME: *15 minutes*
COOKING TIME: *10 minutes*
MAKES *18 muffins*

1½ *cups flour*
1 *cup yellow cornmeal*
½ *teaspoon salt*
4 *teaspoons baking powder*
¼ *cup sugar*
2 *eggs*
¼ *cup oil*
1 *cup creamed corn*
¾ *cup milk*
1 *tablespoon chopped parsley*

1 Preheat oven to 210°C. Grease well two deep patty pan trays. Sift flour, cornmeal, salt, baking powder and sugar into a large mixing bowl. In a large jug lightly beat eggs, oil, creamed corn, and milk and parsley together to combine.
2 Make a well in the centre of the dry ingredients and pour in the liquid ingredients. Mix quickly with a fork to combine all ingredients. Do not overmix.
3 Spoon into muffin tins and bake immediately in preheated oven about 10 minutes. Serve warm.

Country Milk Rolls

These small, tender rolls are enriched by the addition of full-cream milk powder and sprinkled with tasty poppy seeds. They are delicious served warm with butter or jam.

PREPARATION TIME: *25 minutes + 1 hour standing*
COOKING TIME: *15 minutes*
MAKES *12 rolls*

1 x 7 g *dry yeast sachet*
1 *teaspoon sugar*
1¾ *cups lukewarm water*
4 *cups plain flour*
⅓ *cup full cream milk powder*

1 *egg for glazing*
2 *tablespoons poppy seeds*

1 Combine yeast, sugar and water in a jug or basin and stand in sink of warm water until mixture starts to bubble, about 10 minutes.
2 Sift flour and milk powder into large basin, make a well in the centre, add yeast mixture and stir to form a soft dough. Knead until smooth and elastic. Place in lightly oiled basin, cover with plastic film and leave in a warm place until dough is doubled in bulk.
3 Punch down; knead lightly. Divide mixture into 12 even pieces and shape into smooth round balls. Place on lightly greased baking trays in warm position until well risen.
4 Brush each roll with lightly beaten egg and sprinkle with poppy seeds. Bake at 180°C for 15 minutes. Serve warm with butter or jam.

Crisp Almond Rounds

An excellent addition to cheeseboards or to serve with spreads or dips, this small crisp flatbread has a strong, nutty flavour.

PREPARATION TIME: *40 minutes*
COOKING TIME: *12 minutes*
MAKES *36 rounds*

Country Milk Rolls

1 *cup almonds, toasted and ground*
2 *cups plain flour*
1 *tablespoon sugar*
½ *teaspoon baking powder*
2 *tablespoons melted butter*
¾ *cup buttermilk*

1 Combine almonds, flour, sugar and baking powder.
2 Make well in centre and add melted butter and buttermilk. Mix well.
3 Place dough on lightly floured board and knead until smooth, about 2–3 minutes. Roll into sausage shape and cut into 36 equal portions. Knead each piece into ball. Roll out into 6 cm round.
4 Place on ungreased baking tray. Bake at 180°C for 10–12 minutes. Cool on tray. Serve warm or cold.

English Muffins

Up until the 1930s the muffin man was a familiar sight around the streets of London. Muffins are like cake in texture and resemble the 'baps' of Scotland.

PREPARATION TIME: *20 minutes + 1½–2 hours rising time*
COOKING TIME: *12–15 minutes*
MAKES *10 muffins*

2½ cups plain flour
1 teaspoon salt
1 teaspoon sugar
300 mL warm water
15 g fresh yeast or 7 g dried yeast
1 tablespoon olive oil

1 Dissolve the sugar in warm water and add the yeast. Stir to combine. Cover and set aside for about 10 minutes or until the mixture froths.
2 Sift the flour and salt into a large bowl. Make a well in the centre of the flour, pour in the yeast mixture and olive oil. Mix vigorously to blend in the flour. The dough should be soft but still hold its shape. Knead to a smooth elastic dough, about 15 minutes. Place in a greased bowl, cover and place in a warm place to rise for about 35–40 minutes. It should double in bulk.
3 Turn out the dough onto a floured surface, knead lightly and cut into 10 even pieces. Mould the pieces into balls, dust with flour and cover. Set aside to rise again about 30 minutes.
4 Heat a griddle, hotplate or heavy-based frying pan and oil it lightly. Carefully lift the dough pieces onto the heated griddle. Cook two at a time for 5–6 minutes. Turn and cook the second side about 6 minutes. Muffins should be pulled apart with the fingers, toasted slowly on both sides and well buttered.

English Muffins

Yeast is a traditional raising agent known since earliest times. It is available commercially for bread baking in two forms. Fresh or compressed yeast, available from health food stores and some bakeries, is in block form, creamy in colour, cool to touch and crumbly when broken. The aroma is pleasant, not sour. Store in the refrigerator. Dried yeast comes in the form of dry granules, usually sold in a packet with individual sachets inside, each sachet weighing 7 g. Check 'use-by' dates before purchasing. Store in a cool dry place.

Italian Focaccia

Focaccia is a chewy Italian bread that can be used as an antipasto treat. It serves also as a bread base for pizza type toppings. It can be plain, garlic or anchovy flavoured.

PREPARATION TIME: *35 minutes + 1¼ hours standing*
COOKING TIME: *25 minutes*
MAKES *2 rectangular breads*

1 tablespoon sugar
2 cups warm water
1 sachet dry yeast (7 g)
5 cups plain flour
2 tablespoons olive oil
1 teaspoon salt
⅓ cup olive oil, extra
1 clove garlic, crushed
2 medium white onions, thinly sliced
1 teaspoon coarse salt

1 In a large bowl dissolve the sugar in warm water. Stir in yeast; let stand in a warm place until frothy, about 10 minutes.
2 Add 4 cups of flour to the yeast mixture with 2 tablespoons oil and 1 teaspoon salt and beat with a wooden spoon until well mixed. (The 5th cup of flour is used up in the kneading.) Turn mixture out onto a floured surface and knead until mixture is smooth, glossy and elastic, about 10 minutes. Place in a clean greased bowl and cover with towel or plastic wrap. Leave in a warm place about 1 hour or until the dough is doubled in bulk.
3 Combine crushed garlic and extra olive oil. In a separate bowl combine onions and coarse salt and set aside.
4 Preheat oven to 220°C and grease two 30 × 25 cm trays.
5 Punch down yeast mixture and divide into two equal balls. Roll out each piece to form a 30 × 25 cm rectangle. Lift and place onto well greased trays. Cover and let stand 15 minutes.
6 Using the handle of a wooden spoon press dough all over to form indents about 1 cm deep. Brush over with garlic oil and sprinkle with half the onion mixture. Repeat with other half of the dough. Bake at 220°C until crisp and golden.
7 Cut into pieces to serve.

Crisp Almond Rounds (page 85) and Italian Focaccia

Barley Round and Sesame Flatbreads

Barley Round

This is an unusual scone-like dough that contains cooked barley. The addition of buttermilk combines with the raising agent to give a light, tender dough. Barley Round freezes well for up to three months.

PREPARATION TIME: *35 minutes*
COOKING TIME: *25 minutes*
MAKES *1 x 30 cm round*

2 *cups plain flour*
1 *cup rye flour*
2 *teaspoons sugar*
2 *teaspoons baking powder*
½ *teaspoon bicarbonate of soda*
½ *cup raw pearl barley*
60 *g butter, melted*
1¼ *cups buttermilk*
extra milk for glazing.

1 Cook barley in boiling water until tender. Drain and allow to cool.
2 Sift flour, sugar, baking powder and bicarbonate of soda into large mixing bowl. Add cooked barley. Mix well.
3 Make well in centre. Add combined butter and buttermilk. Stir to form a soft dough.
4 Turn onto lightly floured board. Press dough into lightly oiled 30 cm pizza pan.
5 Glaze with extra milk. Bake at 200°C for 20–25 minutes.
6 Serve warm, cut into wedges.

Crispy Seeded Flatbreads

Crisp flatbread that can be broken into pieces is ideal to serve with dips and pâtés or to top with your favourite spread.

PREPARATION TIME: *45 minutes + 1 hour standing*
COOKING TIME: *15 minutes*
MAKES *4 large flatbreads*

¾ *cup warm water*
3 *egg whites, unbeaten*
1 *tablespoon melted butter*
1 *teaspoon salt*
1 *teaspoon sugar*
1 *teaspoon dry yeast*

2 cups plain flour
1 tablespoon poppy seeds
1 teaspoon sesame seeds
1 teaspoon caraway seeds

1 Combine water, egg whites, melted butter, salt, sugar and yeast. Stand 5 minutes.
2 Sift flour into large bowl, make well in centre and pour in yeast mixture. Beat to form a soft dough.
3 Place dough on floured surface and knead until it holds its shape. Place in lightly oiled basin, brush top with oil and cover with plastic wrap. Place in warm position until doubled in bulk.
4 Punch dough down. Divide into four even pieces. Knead each until smooth and shiny. Roll each piece into large 3 mm thick round and prick all over with a fork. Brush with water and sprinkle with combined seeds.
5 Place on lightly oiled baking tray. Bake at 200°C for 10–15 minutes until bread is golden brown.

Wholemeal Rye Sourdough Bread

This is a delicious wholemeal and rye bread made with a sourdough starter, which gives a distinctive, slightly acid flavour. The sourdough starter needs two days to ferment at room temperature. It can be stored for six to seven days in the refrigerator thereafter.

PREPARATION TIME: *50 minutes*
COOKING TIME: *40 minutes*
MAKES *1 large or 2 small loaves*

SOURDOUGH STARTER
5 g fresh yeast
1 cup warm water
1 cup wholemeal flour
BREAD DOUGH
1½ cups water
30 g fresh yeast
2 teaspoons brown sugar
2½ cups rye flour
2 teaspoons caraway seeds
extra rye flour for kneading

1 To make the sourdough starter, dissolve yeast in warm water. Sift in flour and mix until smooth. Cover bowl and leave to stand at room temperature for 2 days.
2 For the bread dough, combine water, yeast and brown sugar. Leave to stand in warm place until mixture starts to bubble.
3 Place rye flour in large basin. Make well in centre and add yeast mixture and ½ cup sourdough starter. Mix until well combined. Knead until dough is smooth and elastic. Place in lightly oiled basin and leave in warm position until doubled in bulk.
4 Punch dough down, place on floured surface and knead for 10 minutes. Shape into one or two long, oval-shaped loaves. Place on greased tray and allow to prove 10 minutes. Glaze with water and sprinkle with caraway seeds. Bake at 200°C for 30–40 minutes until golden brown.

Wholemeal Rye Sourdough Bread

Sesame Flatbreads

In this soft sesame-coated flatbread, wholemeal flour may be substituted for white. It will add increased fibre content and a slight nutty flavour.

PREPARATION TIME: *45 minutes + 1 hour standing time*
COOKING TIME: *25 minutes*
MAKES *4 flatbreads*

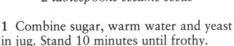

1 tablespoon sugar
2 cups warm water
1 x 7 g sachet dry yeast
4 cups plain flour
2 tablespoons olive oil
milk for glazing
2 tablespoons sesame seeds

1 Combine sugar, warm water and yeast in jug. Stand 10 minutes until frothy.
2 Sift flour into large basin and make well in centre. Add yeast mixture and oil. Beat until well combined.
3 Place dough on floured surface and knead until smooth and glossy. Place in lightly oiled basin, brush with oil and cover with plastic wrap. Stand in warm place until double in bulk.
4 Punch dough down. Divide into 4 even pieces and knead each into a ball. Shape each into 30 cm oval, brush with milk and sprinkle with sesame seeds. Stand 10 minutes. Bake at 180°C for 20–25 minutes.
5 Cool on wire racks. Tear into pieces for serving.

When a bread dough has been kneaded sufficiently the dough develops elasticity. To test for elasticity press the ball of dough gently with a finger. If the indentation springs back the dough is said to be 'elastic'.

JAMS, JELLIES AND PRESERVES

Jam is made by boiling together sugar and fruit to form a sugar concentration high enough to preserve the mixture and prevent spoilage. A good jam should be set to a firm consistency and have a fine clear colour, characteristic of the fruit in the jam. It should be neither too sweet nor too acid. Jellies are made on the same principle as jams but the fruit is strained so that a clear, full-flavoured jelly results. Conserves are very similar to jams except that the fruit remains firm, retaining its original shape. Conserves are best made with soft berry or stone fruits.

What makes jams, jellies and conserves set is the combination of sugar, pectin and acid. The last two both occur naturally in fruit but to varying degrees. It is for this reason that some fruits are combined with other fruits to create a balance that will give a good setting quality.

Essential Points for Jam

Choose fruit that is slightly under-ripe, because it has the highest ratio of pectin and acid to sugar. Remove any damaged sections of fruit, wash and dry with absorbent paper.

Unless the recipe states otherwise use white crystal sugar which gives a clear result in jams and jellies.

You will need a large saucepan with a heavy base, glass bowls and metal and wooden spoons. A sugar thermometer is an asset when checking the setting point; when the thermometer reaches 105°C the jam has reached setting point. If a thermometer is not available use the saucer test. Simply place a saucer in the freezer until it is very cold, place a little jam on the saucer and leave it undisturbed to become cold. Use a spoon or your finger and gently push the jam. If the surface appears wrinkly with a skin on the surface the jam is ready. If the jam is still runny, continue to boil mixture until setting point is reached.

Jars must be sterilised to prevent the growth of micro-organisms. After ensuring jars are thoroughly cleaned, rinse in very hot water and place upside down on a rack to drain. Warm jars in a very slow oven (150°C) and use jars straight from the oven. Lids should be boiled or rinsed in very hot water and allowed to drain.

Ensure jams, jellies and conserves are sealed correctly, as a good seal is essential in keeping the preserve in optimum condition. You can use a plastic or plastic coated metal lid, melted wax or cellophane jam covers.

Remember to label and date preserves at the time of making.

Tomato Passionfruit Jam

This Tomato Passionfruit Jam makes a Swiss roll with a difference.

Unroll freshly baked cool Swiss roll. Whip 300 mL sour cream until fluffy and fold through ½ cup Tomato Passionfruit Jam. Spread over Swiss roll and reroll. Serve with extra cream and fresh passionfruit.

PREPARATION TIME: *20 minutes*
COOKING TIME: *1½ hours*
MAKES *1 litre*

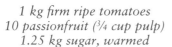

1 kg firm ripe tomatoes
10 passionfruit (¾ cup pulp)
1.25 kg sugar, warmed

1 Wash, peel and coarsely chop tomatoes. Remove pulp from passionfruit and put half the skins into a saucepan, add enough water to cover and cook briskly 20 minutes or until skins are soft inside. Using a teaspoon, scoop out all the softened white inner skin, put this aside and discard the outer skins.
2 Put tomatoes and passionfruit pulp into a large saucepan or boiler and bring to boiling point.
3 Add the scrapings from the skins and the warmed sugar and stir until sugar has dissolved. Boil rapidly, stirring frequently until setting point is reached.
4 Remove cooked jam from heat and stand 1–2 minutes. Pour into warm, sterilised jars and seal immediately. When cool, label and date.

1 Simmer fruit in a large saucepan or boiler until soft and pulpy.

2 Suspend muslin cloth between the legs of an upturned stool. Strain fruit.

3 Place juice in saucepan, boil, add sugar and stir until sugar dissolves.

4 Test setting point by placing a little jelly on a cold saucer. When cold jelly should wrinkle.

Blackberry and Apple Jelly

When buying blackberries look for firm, plump fruit.

A delicious serving suggestion is to pan-fry 4 flour-coated chicken breasts. Remove and keep warm. Stir in ½ cup Blackberry and Apple Jelly to deglaze pan, simmer 1 minute and stir in ¼ cup cream. Pour over chicken and serve.

PREPARATION TIME: *20 minutes*
COOKING TIME: *1¾ hours*
MAKES *2.5 litres*

3 x 250 g punnets blackberries
6 medium green apples
4 medium pears
⅔ cup lemon juice
sugar

1 Wash blackberries, apples and pears and drain. Finely chop apples and pears, including cores and seeds.
2 Combine blackberries with chopped fruit in a large saucepan or boiler and cover with water. Bring to boil and simmer, covered, for about 1 hour or until fruit is soft and pulpy.
3 Strain fruit and liquid through muslin bag suspended over a bowl for 3 hours. Measure juice and return to saucepan. Stir in lemon juice. Heat until boiling. Add ¾ cup sugar per cup of juice. Return to boil, stirring until sugar dissolves. Boil rapidly, uncovered, for about 40–45 minutes or until setting point is reached.
4 Remove cooked jelly from heat and stand 5 minutes. Pour into warm, sterilised jars and cool completely before sealing. When cook, label and date.

Cakes, Biscuits & Puddings

THE SUGAR-AND-SPICE FLAVOURS of sweet cakes and puddings promise happy endings to savoury menus. Plan a meal crowned with Coffee Hazelnut Custard, an enticing old French dish; offer slices of Sweet Fruity Country Cake, Apple Sauce Cake, Spanish Syrup Biscuits or any of the other irresistible confections we present for your selection. They are all created from simple, available ingredients, just as they would have been in the past. These old-fashioned sweet things never go out of favour and are always sure to delight your family and friends. Serve them with coffee or a glass of wine and congratulate the cook.

Sweet Polenta Cake (page 104), Figs in Syrup (page 98) and Berry Tart (page 95)

Raspberries are the fruit of a shrub from the rose family, native to Northern Canada, Northern USA, Europe and Scandinavia. The aggregate of one-seeded fruits is massed together round a single hull. The most common raspberry is deep red in colour, with black and yellow raspberries found mainly in Canada and the USA. The season is usually very short, so enjoy these fruits when you can at their seasonal best.

Sweet Fruity Country Cake

This cake has an unusual texture as it is made of breadcrumbs instead of flour. Take special care to beat the egg whites thoroughly to ensure an even-textured cake. The dried fruit keeps the cake moist for several days. Store covered in the refrigerator or in an airtight container.

PREPARATION TIME: *30 minutes*
COOKING TIME: *45 minutes*
MAKES *1 x 25 cm cake*

100 g sultanas
100 g dried figs
2 tablespoons cognac
2 tablespoons orange juice
60 g soft dried apricots
30 g butter
5 cups crustless wholemeal breadcrumbs

8 eggs, separated
1 cup caster sugar
2 teaspoons grated orange rind
300 mL whipped sweetened cream and
½ cup finely chopped dried figs or
icing sugar for decoration

1 Soak sultanas and figs in combined cognac and orange juice for 20 minutes. Finely chop dried apricots.
2 Preheat oven to 170°C. Grease a 25 cm springform pan with the butter, using all 30 g. Scatter over half a cup of the breadcrumbs.
3 Beat the egg yolks and sugar together until thick and creamy. Add grated orange rind. Fold through breadcrumbs and fruit.
4 Beat egg whites until soft peaks form. Fold through fruit mixture. Pour into prepared cake pan.
5 Bake in preheated oven until cooked, about 45 minutes. Stand 30 minutes before turning out. Cool.
6 Decorate with whipped cream and figs or sifted icing sugar.

1 Grease a 25 cm springform pan with the butter, using all 30 g. Scatter ½ cup of the breadcrumbs evenly over the base and sides of the pan.

2 Using a small bowl and an electric mixer beat the egg yolks and sugar together until mixture is thick and creamy. Add the grated orange rind.

3 Using a clean large bowl beat egg whites with an electric mixer until soft peaks form.

4 Gently fold fruit and breadcrumb mixture through egg white mixture.

Berry Tart

This is a French open tart, using berries in season. The pastry is baked blind and the fruit prepared separately. When the pastry is cool it is filled with drained fruit and returned to the oven for 5 minutes. This prevents the pastry from being sodden.

PREPARATION TIME: *20 minutes + 1 hour chilling time*
COOKING TIME: *30 minutes*
MAKES *1 x 23 cm tart*

PASTRY
1½ cups plain flour
90 g butter
½ cup sugar
3 egg yolks
¼ teaspoon vanilla essence
FILLING
2 punnets raspberries
1 punnet blueberries or blackcurrants
½ cup sugar
3 tablespoons redcurrant jelly

1 Sift flour into basin, make well in centre and add butter, sugar, egg yolks and vanilla essence. Using fingertips, work them together. Mix the dough to a ball. Put pastry onto lightly floured surface and knead lightly. Wrap in plastic film and chill for 1 hour before using.
2 Roll out pastry between 2 sheets of greaseproof paper, turning and lifting paper to ensure there are no creases in pastry. Line a greased 23 cm fluted flan tin with pastry, being careful not to stretch pastry. Ease gently into tin, trim edges. Chill for 10 minutes. Blind bake at 180°C for 15–20 minutes or until pastry is a pale biscuit colour. Cool.
3 Wash berries, place in saucepan with sugar and cook covered on low heat for 5–7 minutes until sugar has dissolved. Strain fruit; reserve liquid. Cool fruit.
4 Place fruit in cooled pastry case. Bake at 180°C for 5 minutes. Combine reserved liquid and redcurrant jelly in small saucepan and heat until redcurrant jelly is dissolved. Cool slightly. Spoon glaze over fruit.
5 Serve warm or cold.

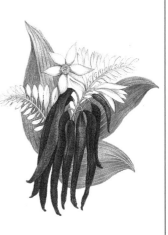

Sweet Fruity Country Cake

Poppy-seed Torte

This unusual torte is Polish in origin and combines poppy seeds and chocolate to complement a short almond pastry.

PREPARATION TIME: 35 minutes
COOKING TIME: 50–60 minutes
MAKES 1 x 20 cm torte

PASTRY
1½ cups flour
⅓ cup sugar
100 g ground almonds
125 g butter
1 egg
FILLING
200 g poppy seeds, crushed in blender
150 mL milk
½ cup sugar
100 g dark chocolate, grated
½ cup raisins, chopped
50 g ground almonds
1 egg, lightly beaten
extra egg for glaze
1 tablespoon poppy seeds, extra

Poppy seeds are small grey-black seeds from the opium poppy, native to the Middle East. Before grinding, they are best lightly toasted.

1 To make pastry, combine all dry ingredients in food processor, turn motor on and add butter. When butter is evenly mixed, add egg and blend to bring pastry together. Wrap in plastic wrap and chill while preparing the filling.
2 To make filling, place poppy seeds in a small saucepan, add milk and heat slowly to bring milk to the boil; reduce heat and simmer 5 minutes. Remove from heat and add sugar, cool slightly and then stir through the grated chocolate. Mix through ground almonds and beaten egg. Allow mixture to cool.
3 Cut chilled pastry into three parts. Roll each third into a 20 cm disc. Press one third onto the base of a greased 20 cm torte pan. Spread over half the poppy seed mixture, then another disc, remaining poppy seed mixture and lastly the remaining pastry disc. Use a little beaten egg to glaze and scatter extra poppy seeds over top. Bake at 180°C for about 45 minutes or until golden and crisp.

Spanish Syrup Biscuits

These crisp pastries may be either disc-shaped or cut into finger-sized pieces with a fluted pastry cutter.

PREPARATION TIME: 45 minutes + 2½ hours standing
COOKING TIME: 20 minutes
MAKES 25 pastries

1 cup water
2 tablespoons sugar
½ teaspoon salt
2 teaspoons grated orange rind
4 cups plain flour
2 teaspoons baking powder
125 g butter
1 egg, lightly beaten
oil for deep frying
ORANGE SYRUP
1 cup brown sugar
½ cup water
1 teaspoon grated orange rind
1 stick cinnamon

1 Put water, sugar, salt and orange rind into a saucepan and heat gently until sugar melts. Cool till lukewarm.
2 Sift flour and baking powder into a bowl and rub in butter until mixture resembles fine breadcrumbs. Add the beaten egg and warm sugared water. Work to a soft dough and knead well for at least 15 minutes until the dough is smooth, glossy and elastic. Press into a long roll, cover and refrigerate for at least 2 hours.
3 Slice into 25 even-sized pieces. Work with one piece of dough at a time. Keep remaining pieces covered to prevent drying out. Roll out pastry to form a disc: the pastry should be so thin as to be almost transparent. Place on a tray to dry and continue with remaining pieces of dough. Stand pastry 30 minutes before frying or until pastry has a dry outer surface.
4 Prepare syrup by combining syrup ingredients and cooking over a low heat until sugar dissolves. Increase heat and simmer until mixture becomes syrupy.
5 Deep-fry pastries one at a time; the pastry should blister and cook in a few seconds. Lift out and drain on absorbent paper.
6 Dip into warm syrup just before serving or serve plain, dusted with icing sugar.

Glazed Yoghurt Spice Cake (page 98), Spanish Syrup Biscuits and Poppyseed Torte

Glazed Yoghurt Spice Cake

A delightfully flavoured, moist cake that does not have a traditional icing but a buttery, sticky glaze that adds to the moistness of the cake. It is suitable as a dessert cake. Serve with a dollop of plain yoghurt or whipped cream.

PREPARATION TIME: *25 minutes*
COOKING TIME: *60 minutes*
MAKES *1 x 20 cm cake*

1 cup pecans, roughly chopped
1 cup prunes, pitted and chopped
2 cups self-raising flour
1 teaspoon bicarbonate of soda
1 teaspoon cinnamon
1 teaspoon nutmeg
2 teaspoons mixed spice
1 cup sugar
½ cup vegetable oil
1 cup low-fat plain yoghurt
3 eggs
1 teaspoon vanilla essence
a little desiccated coconut
GLAZE
¼ cup brown sugar
¼ cup low-fat plain yoghurt
2 tablespoons butter
1 teaspoon vanilla essence
1 teaspoon cinnamon

1 Combine pecans and prunes with ½ cup of flour.
2 Sift together remaining flour, soda and spices. Place in large bowl of electric mixer. Add remaining ingredients except coconut and beat on medium speed for 1 minute or until well combined.
3 Fold combined pecan, prune and flour mixture carefully into cake mixture. Pour mixture into well oiled 20 cm baba or fluted ring tin. For extra insurance against cake sticking, and for extra flavour, after oiling tin, coat it with desiccated coconut.
4 Bake at 160°C for 50–60 minutes or until cake springs back when touched and is dark golden brown. Allow to stand 5 minutes in tin before turning out onto wire rack.
5 Combine all glaze ingredients in small saucepan. Cook over medium heat, stirring occasionally, until butter melts and mixture boils.

6 Place cake on serving plate. Pour glaze over top, allowing some to drizzle down sides. Sprinkle with cinnamon. Allow cake to cool before serving with spoonfuls of yoghurt or lightly whipped cream.

Figs in Syrup

An easy-to-prepare, deliciously sweet dessert that can be served warm or cold. The addition of cinnamon and orange flower water gives it a truly Middle Eastern flavour. The figs may be fully prepared two or three days before they are needed and served chilled.

PREPARATION TIME: *30 minutes + 3 hours soaking*
COOKING TIME: *25 minutes*
SERVES 6

500 g dried figs
3 cups cold tea
¾ cup sugar
1½ cups water
½ cup orange juice
¼ cup honey
thin strip orange rind
1 whole cinnamon stick
1 teaspoon orange flower water
⅓ cup slivered almonds
200 g plain yoghurt

1 Wash figs, cover with cold tea and leave to soak for 3 hours. Remove figs and discard tea.
2 Heat sugar, water and orange juice in heavy-based saucepan, stirring occasionally until sugar has dissolved. Add honey, orange rind and cinnamon stick. Bring to the boil.
3 Add prepared figs and boil gently for 5 minutes. Reduce heat and simmer uncovered for 20 minutes until figs are tender and syrup is reduced. For a thicker syrup, remove figs and allow syrup to cook until required consistency. Remove orange rind and cinnamon stick. Stir in orange flower water.
4 Place figs in serving bowl. Pour over syrup and sprinkle with almonds. Serve with yoghurt.

Are you craving a creamy topping on your favourite dessert, but on a low fat diet? Top with a spoonful of low-fat plain yoghurt whipped lightly with vanilla essence.

Bourbon Bon-Bon Cake

This is a rich fruit and nut cake, which must be left to mature for 1–2 weeks before eating. Scotch whisky can be substituted for bourbon if preferred.

PREPARATION TIME: *30 minutes + 1 hour standing*
COOKING TIME: *2 hours*
MAKES *1 x 20 cm cake*

1 cup raisins
1 cup bourbon
250 g unsalted butter
1 cup brown sugar
4 eggs
3 cups plain flour
1 teaspoon baking powder
1 teaspoon nutmeg
1 teaspoon cinnamon
1 teaspoon ginger
2½ cups coarsely chopped hazelnuts
1 cup glacé cherries, halved
1 cup chopped glacé pineapple
¾ cup jam
2 teaspoons grated orange rind
2 teaspoons grated lemon rind
¼ cup bourbon, extra
½ cup whole glacé cherries, extra
3 slices glacé pineapple, extra

1 Combine raisins and bourbon and allow to stand 1 hour. Drain raisins; reserve bourbon.
2 Cream butter and brown sugar until light and fluffy. Add eggs one at a time, beating well between each addition.
3 Sift flour, baking powder and spices together. Add prepared fruit. Combine creamed butter and sugar mixture with flour and fruit mixture; add reserved bourbon, jam and rind. Stir well to combine.
4 Place mixture in 20 cm square or round tin lined with brown paper. Bake at 150°C for 1¾ hours or till done. Cool in tin.
5 Moisten a 50 cm square of muslin with extra bourbon and wrap cake. Then wrap in aluminium foil or place in plastic bag. Place in refrigerator for 1–2 weeks before eating. During this time, re-moisten cloth with extra bourbon. Decorate with extra cherries and pineapple before serving.

Bourbon Bon-Bon Cake

Eggs are one of our most complete foods. They are a valuable source of protein, fat and vitamins A, D, E, K and B. Eggs are best stored in the refrigerator, but should be removed and brought to room temperature before using.

Italian Almond and Pistachio Biscuits

These Tuscan biscuits are hard and dry in texture. They store well and are used to serve with sweet sherry or coffee.

PREPARATION TIME: *35 minutes*
COOKING TIME: *40 minutes*
MAKES *30 biscuits*

100 g almonds
100 g shelled pistachio nuts
2 cups flour
2 eggs
1 cup caster sugar
1 teaspoon vanilla
½ teaspoon baking powder
pinch salt

To toast almonds, place on baking tray and toast at 180°C until golden brown. Allow to cool before grinding in blender. If a blender is unavailable, almonds may be chopped finely.

1 Preheat oven to 190°C and grease three biscuit trays. Toast the almonds until golden and chop roughly. Cut pistachio nuts in halves.
2 Sift the flour into a bowl, make a well in the centre, add lightly beaten eggs, sugar, vanilla, baking powder and salt. Work with the hands to form a smooth dough. Roll the dough into long finger length pieces. Place on greased tray.
3 Bake in preheated oven for 10–15 minutes. Remove and cool slightly. While still warm, cut into diagonal slices 1 cm thick. Return to baking trays and cook slices for a further 25 minutes or until they are brown.

Italian Almond and Pistachio Biscuits

Almond and Fruit Rice Cake

A deliciously sweet substantial dessert or snack. Do not wash rice before cooking — the starch is needed to produce a thick, creamy consistency.

PREPARATION TIME: *40 minutes*
COOKING TIME: *30 minutes*
MAKES *1 x 20 cm cake*

600 mL milk
½ cup sugar
1 cup short-grain white rice
3 eggs, lightly beaten

¼ teaspoon almond essence
¼ cup candied peel
½ cup chopped dried or glacé figs
¼ cup slivered almonds
1 tablespoon unsalted butter
grated rind of 1 lemon
1 teaspoon cinnamon
4 whole figs and 8 whole toasted almonds, extra, for decoration.

1 Bring milk and sugar to the boil in heavy-based saucepan.
2 Stir in rice. Simmer, stirring occasionally, until all milk has been absorbed.
3 Remove from heat and allow to cool. Add eggs, essence, peel, figs, almonds, butter, rind and cinnamon. Stir to combine.
4 Put mixture into greased and foil-lined 20 cm round cake tin. Bake at 180°C for 25–30 minutes. Turn out onto serving plate. Decorate with extra figs and almonds. Serve warm or cold with lightly whipped cream.

Coffee Hazelnut Custard

This robust coffee-flavoured custard relies on good quality coffee beans. Serve it with a chocolate sauce, whipped cream and fresh seasonal berries.

PREPARATION TIME: *35 minutes + 30 minutes infusion + overnight chilling*
COOKING TIME: *45 minutes*
SERVES 6

½ cup hazelnuts
½ cup crystal sugar
2 cups milk
½ cup whole coffee beans
300 mL cream
¼ cup icing sugar
3 eggs
3 egg yolks

1 Place hazelnuts and sugar in a wide, heavy-based saucepan. Heat gently without stirring until sugar forms a caramel toffee. Tilt the pan occasionally to ensure toffee is not catching on base of pan. Pour onto an oiled tray and allow to cool. Blend in a blender or processor to form praline powder.
2 Crush the coffee beans by placing them in a plastic bag and cracking them with a

rolling pin. Pour milk into a saucepan, add the beans and slowly bring milk to the boil. Stand to infuse 30 minutes; strain.

3 Combine cream, icing sugar, eggs and yolks. Pour over infused milk and blend through custard with hazelnut praline.

4 Lightly butter a 16 cm ovenproof dish and pour in milk mixture. Place dish in baking pan with enough boiling water to come half-way up side of pan. Bake in a moderately slow oven (160°) for about 45 minutes or until custard has set. Stand several hours to cool and refrigerate overnight. Cut into wedges to serve.

Coffee Hazelnut Custard and Almond and Fruit Rice Cake

Apple Sauce Cake, Golden Indian Bread Pudding (page 105) Dried Fruit Salad

Apple Sauce Cake

This unusual moist apple cake has a delicate cardamom flavour. The cake is best made several hours before it is required. It holds a moist texture for several days. Store it in an airtight container.

PREPARATION TIME: *30 minutes*
COOKING TIME: *1 hour*
MAKES *1 x 20 cm cake*

3 cups plain flour
1 teaspoon baking powder
2 teaspoons bicarbonate of soda
2 teaspoons ground cardamom
½ teaspoon salt
185 g butter
2 teaspoons grated lemon rind
2 cups brown sugar
3 eggs
2 cups unsweetened apple sauce
1 cup currants
100 g dried apples, finely chopped
ICING
2 cups icing sugar
2 tablespoons apple sauce
1 teaspoon lemon juice
1 teaspoon melted butter

1 Grease and line a 20 cm springform tin. Preheat oven to 180°C.
2 Sift together flour, baking powder, bicarbonate of soda, cardamom and salt.
3 Cream butter until soft and gradually add sugar, beating well after each addition. Continue beating until mixture is light and fluffy. Add lemon rind and eggs, one at a time, until well combined.
4 Fold through half the sifted flour, then half the apple sauce, the other half sifted flour, then remaining apple sauce. Fold through currants and dried apples.
5 Pour into prepared cake tin and bake for 1 hour or until cooked.
6 Cool and glaze with icing.
7 To make the Icing, sift icing sugar into a bowl and blend in apple sauce, lemon juice and melted butter until mixture is a good smooth consistency.

Dried Fruit Salad

During the winter months when fresh fruit is hard to come by, try this delicious Middle Eastern dried fruit salad.

PREPARATION TIME: *20 minutes + 2 hours chilling time*
COOKING TIME: *15 minutes*
SERVES 6

12 cardamom pods
100 g dried figs
100 g dried pears
100 g dried apples
200 g dried apricots
100 g muscatel raisins
100 g pitted dessert prunes
1 teaspoon orange flower water
1 cup toasted slivered almonds
YOGHURT CARDAMOM CREAM
200 mL plain yoghurt
200 mL sour cream
2 tablespoons brown sugar
¼ teaspoon ground cardamom

1 Tie cardamom pods in a piece of muslin and lightly roll with a rolling pin to bruise the pods.
2 Cut figs and pears into halves. Combine all the fruits in a large saucepan and cover with water, allowing 2 cm above the fruit. Bring to boiling point and add cardamom pods. Simmer 10 minutes. Turn heat off and allow to stand with cardamom pods to cool. During this time the fruit will plump and soften.
3 Remove the cardamom pods, spoon fruit into a serving dish and stir through orange flower water. Chill well before serving with Yoghurt Cardamom Cream and sprinkling with toasted almonds.
4 To make the Yoghurt Cardamom Cream, combine yoghurt, sour cream, brown sugar and ground cardamom. Chill before serving.

Always break eggs into a separate container before using to check on freshness, especially if adding the sixth egg to a six-egg omelette.

Always glaze pastry before making a steam hole or slit. Otherwise the glazing will fill the hole and prevent the steam escaping.

Sweet Polenta Cake

This recipe originated in Italy, where polenta is a staple food used in either sweet or savoury dishes. This cake is best eaten warm on the day it is baked.

PREPARATION TIME: *35 minutes*
COOKING TIME: *1½ hours*
MAKES *1 x 20 cm cake*

¼ *cup sultanas*
¼ *cup currants*
½ *cup sherry or Marsala*
½ *cup milk*
½ *cup orange juice*
2 *teaspoons orange rind*
250 *g ricotta cheese*
¾ *cup sugar*
1½ *cups polenta*
1 *teaspoon cinnamon*
icing sugar

1 Soak sultanas and currants in sherry or Marsala for 15 minutes. Drain, reserving sherry or Marsala.
2 Combine sherry or Marsala, milk, orange juice and rind. Beat into ricotta and sugar.
3 Add polenta to ricotta mixture. Add sultanas, currants and cinnamon. Pour into greased, lined 20 cm round cake tin.
4 Bake at 160° for 1¼–1½ hours. Turn out onto serving plate (bottom becomes top). Serve warm, dusted with icing sugar.
Note: Mixture is very thin before baking.

Fruit Bread and Apple Pudding

This layered apple and bread pudding makes use of stale bread. Apple juice and wine give it a delightful tart flavour.

PREPARATION TIME: *25 minutes*
COOKING TIME: *40 minutes*
SERVES 6

12 *slices day-old fruit bread, crusts removed*
½ *cup apple juice*
½ *cup red wine*
4 *large green apples, peeled, cored and sliced into thin wedges*
¾ *cup coarsely chopped walnuts*
2 *tablespoons brown sugar*
1 *teaspoon cinnamon*
1 *tablespoon unsalted butter*
1 *cup sour cream*
3 *tablespoons brown sugar, extra*

1 Put bread into a bowl, pour over half combined juice and wine and stand 5 minutes. Remove bread from bowl. Place 4

Polenta is yellow maize or cornmeal which is finely or coarsely milled. The textured grain is first prepared as a very thick porridge which can be served with rich moist stews or casserole dishes. Alternatively it may be cooled on flat trays, sliced and grilled or fried until golden and served with sautéed meats and poultry.

Fruit Bread and Apple Pudding

slices in base of greased ovenproof dish.

2 Combine apples, walnuts, sugar and cinnamon. Place half mixture on top of bread. Top with 4 slices of bread and place rest of apple mixture on top. Cover with remaining bread. Pour over remaining juice and wine. Dot with butter.

3 Bake at 180°C for 35–40 minutes.

4 Combine sour cream and extra brown sugar. Allow to stand 10 minutes before serving.

5 Serve pudding warm, topped with a spoonful of sour cream topping.

Golden Indian Bread Pudding

This pudding might be described as the Indian version of French toast. It is served as a dessert accompanied by either fresh or stewed fruit.

PREPARATION TIME: *25 minutes*
COOKING TIME: *20 minutes*
SERVES 6

8 thick slices white bread, crusts removed
80 g unsalted butter
4 tablespoons full-cream milk powder
1 tablespoon water
¼ teaspoon powdered saffron or saffron threads
⅓ cup coconut milk
¼ cup sugar
¼ cup thickened cream
½ teaspoon rosewater
¼ cup chopped pistachio nuts
rose petals for decoration

1 Cut bread in half to form triangles. Melt butter in frying pan, add bread and cook until golden brown on both sides. Place in shallow dish. Mix milk powder and water together to make a paste, fry in pan until golden brown, remove and cool.

2 Combine saffron, milk and sugar in saucepan and stir over low heat until sugar dissolves. Pour over bread; leave to soak 3–4 minutes. Remove and drain bread.

3 Combine milk left from soaking, fried powdered milk, cream and rosewater; stir over low heat 1 minute. Add fried bread and cook gently, turning once, until little liquid remains.

4 Arrange on serving platter. Sprinkle over pistachios and rose petals.

Almond Currant Tart

This delicious and simple almond tart has a dry, dense texture, ideal to serve as an afternoon tea treat. Serve with lashings of thick cream.

PREPARATION TIME: *35 minutes*
COOKING TIME: *30–40 minutes*
MAKES *1 x 25 cm tart*

1 cup currants
1 cup hot strong tea
2 tablespoons lemon juice
1 tablespoon sugar
450 g ground almonds
1 cup caster sugar
2 cups plain flour
3 egg whites, lightly beaten
5 egg yolks
2 whole eggs
2 teaspoons grated lemon rind

1 Combine currants, hot tea, lemon juice and 1 tablespoon sugar. Stand 15 minutes, then drain.

2 Grease and line a 25 cm deep flan tin and preheat oven to 180°C.

3 Mix together half the almonds and half the caster sugar, add flour and mix well. Add egg whites, mixing to form a stiff dough. Press half the prepared mixture into base and sides of flan tin. Reserve remainder for top of flan.

4 Beat egg yolks, whole eggs and remaining sugar until thick and fluffy (about 7 minutes beating). Add lemon rind, fold through remaining ground almonds and, lastly, drained currants. Pour filling into lined flan tin.

5 Sprinkle over remaining almond pastry to form a crumble topping. Press down gently. Bake in prepared oven for 30–40 minutes. Cool before serving.

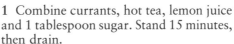

Some recipes call for egg yolks only. Egg whites can be stored for 5 days in a clean glass container in the refrigerator, or frozen for 3–4 weeks. Thaw to room temperature before using.

Almond Currant Tart

Glossary

Although the enjoyment of food is common to all nations, the names by which we know even the most common ingredients can vary from country to country. What Australians call a capsicum is a pepper in England and a bell pepper or sweet pepper in America. To compound the problem, food terms travel – with immigrants, foreign visitors and on food packaging – so even within one country, an item may be known by several different names. Consult the chart to locate an unfamiliar ingredient. Where there is no exact equivalent, an alternative may be suggested.

Fish and meat pose special problems. Because America and Britain share a common ocean, some species of fish are common to both (albeit under different names) but many Australian species are unique. Where possible, recipes describe fish in general rather than specific terms; where a specific type of fish is recommended, a reputable fishmonger will be able to suggest a suitable alternative based upon the cooking method.

There is no standard international method for butchering meat, so cuts vary. The glossary lists some equivalents/substitutes. For more advice, consult your butcher.

Australia	UK	US
Dairy Produce		
cream[1]	single cream	light cream
thickened cream	double cream	heavy cream
sour cream	soured cream	dairy sour cream
lard (animal origin)	lard (animal origin)	use shortening (vegetable origin)
bocconcini	small fresh mozzarella cheeses	small fresh mozzarella cheeses
Romano/Pecorino cheese	Pecorino cheese	Romano cheese
Swiss cheese	Emmenthal cheese	Swiss cheese
tasty cheese	mature Cheddar cheese	sharp Cheddar cheese
eggs, hard-boiled	eggs, hard-boiled	eggs, hard-cooked

[1]The range of creams sold commercially is constantly increasing. Crème fraîche is a cultured thick cream with a slightly sour tang.

Australia	UK	US
Ingredients for Baking		
plain flour	plain flour	all-purpose flour[1]
self-raising flour	self-raising flour	self-rising flour
wholemeal flour	wholemeal flour	Graham/wholewheat flour
cornflour	cornflour	cornstarch
polenta/maize flour	yellow cornmeal	yellow cornmeal
bicarbonate of soda	bicarbonate of soda	baking soda
compressed yeast	fresh yeast	compressed yeast
white crystal sugar	white granulated sugar	white sugar[2]
caster sugar	caster sugar	superfine/extrafine sugar[2]
icing sugar	icing sugar	confectioners'/powdered sugar
demerara sugar	demerara sugar	use light brown sugar
raw sugar	use Muscovado sugar	use Turbinado sugar
golden syrup	golden syrup	use light corn syrup or maple syrup
molasses	use black treacle	molasses

[1]American flour is finely milled – for baking, it may be necessary to add slightly more fat and liquid for similar results. [2]American regular sugar is finer than the UK equivalent; in most instances it can safely be substituted for caster sugar.

Australia	UK	US
Fresh and Dried Fruit, Vegetables, Herbs and Aromatics		
currants	blackcurrants	black currants
custard apple	custard apple	cherimoya[1]
feijoa	feijoa	feijoa/pineapple guava
galangal	[2]	[2]
kiwifruit	kiwifruit	kiwi/Chinese gooseberry
papaya	pawpaw	papaya
passionfruit	passionfruit	passionfruit/purple granadilla
persimmon	use Sharon fruit	persimmon
rambutans[3]	use lychees	use litchis
rock melon	cantaloupe	cantaloupe
tamarillo[4]	tamarillo/tree tomato	tamarillo/tree tomato
glacé cherry	glacé cherry	candied cherry
sultana	sultana	golden/white raisin
aubergine	aubergine	eggplant
beetroot	beetroot	beet
black-eyed bean	black-eyed bean	black-eyed pea
broad bean	broad bean	fava bean/European broad bean
butternut pumpkin	butternut pumpkin	butternut squash
capsicum	pepper	sweet/bell pepper
capsicum (canned pieces/slices)	pimiento	pimiento
celeriac	celeriac	celery root/celeriac/celeri-rave
chick peas	chick peas	garbanzos/chick peas
choko	chayote/christophene	chayote squash
coriander (fresh)	coriander (fresh)	cilantro
cos lettuce	cos lettuce	romaine lettuce
creamed corn (canned)	cream-style corn (canned)	creamed-style corn (canned)
endive/curly endive	endive	chicory
English spinach	spinach	spinach
fennel	fennel	fennel/finocchio
green squash	use pattypan squash	use pattypan squash
haricot beans (dried)	haricot beans (dried)	dried navy beans/Great Northern beans
lamb's lettuce	lamb's lettuce	corn salad
lima beans (dried)	butter beans	lima beans
orange sweet potato/kumara	orange-fleshed sweet potato	sweet potato/yam[5]
potato chips	potato chips	French fries
silver beet	Swiss chard	Swiss chard
snow peas	mangetout	snow peas
snow pea sprouts	use bean sprouts	snow pea sprouts
spring onions	spring onions	scallions
sugar peas	sugarsnaps	sugarsnaps
swede	swede	rutabaga
witloof/chicory	chicory	Belgian endive
zucchini	courgette	zucchini

[1]The term custard apple is used to describe a family of fruit including cherimoya, soursop and sweet sop. [2]Galangal is a rhizome resembling ginger but with a distinctly different flavour. It is not widely known in the UK or the US; ginger can be substituted, but the flavour will not be authentic. [3]Rambutans resemble lychees/litchis in flavour and are sometimes called hairy lychees, because the skin of the small oval fruit is covered with dark red-brown hairy spikes. [4]Tamarillos are smooth-skinned oval fruit, red or yellow in colour. The tough skin must be peeled before use. [5]Although it is customary for Americans to refer to orange-fleshed sweet potatoes as yams, this can cause confusion as true yams are white-fleshed tuberous roots.

Australia	UK	US
Baked Goods and Pastry		
cookie/biscuit	biscuit	cookie
cream cracker	cream cracker	oyster cracker
golden oatmeal biscuits (for crumb crusts)	use digestive biscuits	use Graham crackers
scone	scone	biscuit
sponge finger biscuit	boudoir biscuit	ladyfinger
shortcrust pastry	shortcrust pastry	basic pie dough
filo pastry	filo pastry	phyllo leaves
Nuts, Seeds and Grains		
copha	solid coconut cream	coconut butter
desiccated coconut	desiccated coconut	use shredded coconut
hazelnuts	hazelnuts	filberts/hazelnuts
pine nuts	pine nuts/pine kernels	pignoli/pinenuts
pepitas	dried untoasted pumpkin seeds	dried untoasted pumpkin seeds
burghul	bulgur/parboiled hulled cracked wheat	bulgur
cracked/kibbled wheat	cracked wheat	cracked wheat
Meat and Fish (see also general introduction)		
bacon rashers	bacon rashers	bacon slices/strips
back bacon	back bacon	Canadian bacon
streaky bacon	streaky bacon	bacon[1]
belly of pork	belly of pork	fresh pork sides
blade or round steak	use stewing steak	blade or round steak
boneless chicken breasts	chicken breast fillets	chicken cutlets/suprêmes
cabanossi	smoked sausage with garlic and spices	smoked sausage with garlic and spices
coppa	cured ham[2]	cured ham[2]
corned silverside	salted silverside	corned beef
ham steaks	gammon steaks	ham steaks
kassler	lightly salted pork loin smoked with juniper berries	lightly salted pork smoked with juniper berries or top round
minced meat	minced meat	ground meat[3]
offal	offal	variety meats
pancetta	cured pork sausage	cured pork sausage
pork fillet	pork fillet	pork tenderloin
sausage mince	sausagemeat	sausagemeat
topside roast	beef topside	use round rump roast
king prawns	king prawns	jumbo shrimp
prawns[4]	prawns	shrimp
shrimp	shrimp	baby/cocktail shrimp

[1]Packaged American sliced bacon is cut very thinly; substitute 3 slices for every 2 rashers listed in recipes. [2]Coppa is an Italian cured ham, fattier than Prosciutto, from the shoulder and the neck of the pig. [3]Americans sometimes refer to ground beef as hamburger. [4]The term 'green prawns' is sometimes used to describe raw prawns.

Australia	UK	US
Storecupboard Items		
cooking chocolate	cooking chocolate/Menière	unsweetened baking chocolate
dark chocolate	plain chocolate	semisweet chocolate
milk chocolate	milk chocolate	sweet chocolate
choc bits	use chocolate chips	use chocolate chips
chocolate vermicelli/hail	chocolate vermicelli	chocolate sprinkles
hundreds and thousands	hundreds and thousands	nonpareil
jelly crystals	jelly cubes	flavoured gelatin[1]
shoyu/tamari	naturally fermented soy sauce	naturally fermented soy sauce
stock cubes	stock cubes	bouillon cubes[2]
tomato purée	passata	tomato purée
tomato paste	tomato purée(concentrate)	tomato paste
tomato sauce	thin puréed tomatoes	tomato sauce
vanilla bean	vanilla pod	vanilla bean
vanilla essence	vanilla essence	vanilla extract[3]

[1]Jelly (the dessert, not the preserve) comes as crystals or cubes. Check package instructions when making up in case the amount of liquid required is different from that specified in recipes. [2]Some bouillon cubes are only half the size of regular stock cubes; check the labelling for the amount of liquid to use. [3]Vanilla essence/extract comes in different strengths; add to taste. Use natural vanilla essence where possible.

Appliances, Cookware and Paper Products

absorbent paper	kitchen paper	paper towels
bar pan	loaf tin	loaf pan
double saucepan	double saucepan	double boiler
frying pan	frying pan	skillet
greaseproof paper	greaseproof paper	use waxed paper or baking parchment
griller	grill	broiler[1]
Lamington tin	28 x 18 cm /11 x 7 in baking tray, 4 cm/1½ in deep	28 x 18 cm/11 x 7 in baking tray, 4 cm/1½ in deep
patty cases	paper cake cases	cupcake papers
plastic wrap	cling film	plastic wrap
sandwich cake tin	sandwich cake tin	layer cake pan
springform tin	spring-release tin	springform pan
Swiss roll tin	Swiss roll tin	jelly roll pan
tea-towel	tea-towel	dish-towel
toothpick	cocktail stick	toothpick

[1]Where Australian and British cooks talk about grilling, Americans use the term broiling, except for barbecued food, which is grilled in all three countries.